LAUGHING MATTERS

AN ANATOMY OF MIRTH

LAUGHING MATTERS

AN ANATOMY OF MIRTH

Andrew Herron

LINDSAY
PUBLICATIONS

First Published in 2000 by
Lindsay Publications
Glasgow

Copyright © 2000 Andrew Herron

No part of this publication may be reproduced, stored or transmitted
in any form or by any means, electronic, merhanical, photocopying,
recording or otherwise without the express written permission of
the Publisher

ISBN 1 898169 22 5

British Library Cataloguing-in Publication Date
A CIP record of this book is available from the British Library

Designed and typeset in Garamond 11 on 13 point by
Greative Imprint, Glasgow

Front cover illustration by John Gahagan

Printed and bound in Finland by WS Bookwell

CONTENTS

PREFACE

'Laughing Matters' – of course laughing matters.

It is odd that it should have taken what amounted to a stroke of genius on the part of a lassie in the publisher's office to see how this was our perfect title. I had been wrestling with the title without any real satisfaction and then came the answer to my quest. Please, 'lassie in the publisher's employment', accept my warmest thanks – and that with a happy smile if not with laughter.

It is no laughing matter how many of life's serious problems have been resolved with a joke. Were statistics a possibility I'm sure it would be found that humour has done more to shape the course of human history than all the tears – though the latter have been shed in rich profusion and have always had a splendid press.

Has it ever occurred to you that one reason may be that the joke has no foundation in Scripture – you can search the Testaments in vain if what you are looking for is a witticism – and that is giving it its widest possible interpretation. Why this should be so I just cannot conceive. I could think of many a worse theme for a thesis.

It was in 1950 that I resigned my parish of Houston and Killellan to become full-time Clerk to the Presbytery of Glasgow, an office in which I found a great deal of satisfaction. Around the seventies there was much talk of retiring on account of my age and I was well past the standard mark. There was no obligation on me to go and though still perfectly fit and more than willing to continue I felt I should fall in with my neighbours and so I tendered my resignation.

How was I to put in my time? I had to do something to fill in my day. So I wrote an article which I thought might attract attention and be published. This led to a second article, then a third and so on until we now have the present publication. If you don't enjoy reading it be comforted by the fact that I have had a lot of fun compiling and writing it – and you wouldn't want to grudge me that.

I am much in debt to the Publisher, not only for the title but also for the cover illustration. My first reaction on seeing this was to suggest that a prize might be offered to the first person who identified himself or herself in the drawing. I realised that this would be a complete give-away – the lady with the hat has no competition. This raises another issue – why ladies had to be covered in Church?

I go back something over fifty years to a glorious sunny summer afternoon when I was understudying for the official guide at a lovely wee kirk in the Yorkshire Dales whilst he went off for a well-deserved afternoon break. We were getting along fine when suddenly he reappeared and spotted a girl in the company who was without headgear – he couldn't have been more distressed had she been headless! I am not aware of any legislation changing the official position of the Church yet I attended a service on Sunday at which I detected only three ladies who were wearing a hat.

This was meant to be a preface to a book already written. It has turned out to be a challenge for two others!

ANDREW HERRON
June 2000, Glasgow

CHAPTER ONE

THE FEEBLE PUN

WHAT IS A JOKE? The simplest definition I can find is 'something said or done that excites laughter'. Since our interest is entirely in the joke that is told, we confine ourselves to 'something said that excites laughter'. This seems fair so far as it goes; but is it far enough? We really want to learn what it is about a joke that excites laughter rather than anger or tears, embarrassment or excitement.

The true answer is to be found, I think, in a consideration of the definition of laughter. That, we are told, relates to a 'recognition of the ludicrous'. Quite simply, then, a joke might be said to consist in the narration of circumstances depicting a situation that is ridiculous, or in the manipulation of language in such a way that it produces a ridiculous conclusion. This, I readily grant, is a circular kind of definition, for the questioner is entitled to go on and ask, 'But what do you mean by "ridiculous"?' and that brings you full cycle to 'what excites laughter' and before you know it are back at the joke from which you started. The effort to define a joke becomes itself something of a joke.

If we are to have any hope of reaching an understanding of our subject we must turn aside from the attempt to define a joke in purely theoretical terms and look instead at the subject of humour at a more practical level.

It seems that a joke may fall into one of two classes – the narration of circumstances that depict or lead to a ridiculous situation, or the clever manipulation of language to create the element of the ridiculous. The first of these – the joke situation – may take one of many forms and the bulk of our present exercise consists in an attempt to classify and systematise these in some degree. Let us, however, at this stage think a little about the joke that is essentially an affair of words, and let us begin by taking it in its simplest form.

The simplest form of word-joke – indeed of any joke – is the pun. It is often claimed that the pun is not only the simplest form of humour but it is also the lowest form. Now it is true that we can be subjected to some pretty appalling puns – more appalling than pretty – but this is not so much a condemnation of this humour-form as an indictment of those who reduce it to such levels of depravity. I am interested in Fowler's comment that puns are 'good, bad, and indifferent, and only those who lack the wit to make them are unaware of the fact'.

Let us think for a moment of the pun as a serious contribution to the field of humour. In the pun the humorist produces an amusing result by taking advantage of the fact that one and the same word can have two entirely different meanings – homonyms such as 'bark', which may belong either to a dog or to a tree, 'main', which may be an adjective meaning principal or a noun meaning 'ocean'; or that two words with completely different meanings and spellings happen to sound the same – homophones such as key and quay, bark and barque, place and plaice, site and sight, rain, rein and reign.

The kind of pun based upon the homonym may be illustrated by the simple remark that a friend is training for a job on the railway, or that I came across a tramp who couldn't play bridge because his only decent suit was in pawn, or that I knew a lassie who found her job in Magnet House most attractive. Puns of this kind are subtle rather than just simple, and are not very funny. You have to keep on your toes if you're not to miss them altogether. Not that your life would be immeasurably impoverished if you did miss them altogether – a view not always shared by the happy perpetrator.

The kind of pun built around the homophone was rather neatly illustrated in a conversation I overheard recently. The man was talking to some friends about a house he had taken in the country for a holiday break. On arrival he had found to his horror that instead of the indoor facilities he had been led to expect there was a hut down a garden path. Instantly one of the friends put in, 'O, that would be in lieu'. Or there was the dog called Locksmith because it was always making bolts for the door. Or the definition of a milk-shake as an Arab dairy-farmer on a large scale. Best of all there's the Glasgow classic about laying a carpet, that you need a flair for it.

Normally there is little that is mirth-provoking in the actual situation the pun depicts, the secret of its success is that it has to be instant.

A good deal of what passes for humour on the TV these days is of very poor quality – 'neither guid nor middlin', as we say in the country. As I have tried to indicate, a smart rejoinder in reply to the pun can be highly entertaining but twenty minutes of continuous contrived punning, much of it carrying a strong smell of midnight oil, is wearisome. There seems no limit to the degree of ingenuity which the punster is prepared to invoke – witness the crack about the man who called his dog Tales of Hoffman because it didn't offenbach. That wasn't worth even a raspberry.

To make matters worse – for me at least – the professional wits tend to go in for the kind of pun generally described as *double entendre* (though obviously that is a fair description of any pun). A deliberate ambiguity is conveyed not openly but by a knowing look or a leer or a snigger, because the second meaning is suggestive in character. Its smell is even worse than midnight oil, a little goes a long way. It needn't go a long way – a short trip would take it to the dustbin where it properly belongs.

To return to our nice, simple, uncomplicated pun there's a delightful story I'd like to tell, for it also makes quite a few points about humour generally.

> The morning bus was packed as usual when Eustace joined it *en route* for the office. Scarcely had he stepped into the gangway when the driver engaged gear and Eustace found himself hurled from one end of the passage to the other, to end on the knees of a lady in the front seat. The situation was considerably relieved when a man across the passage greeted him, 'Good morning, Laplander'. In the titter of laughter that ensued, Eustace was able to regain his feet and his composure.
>
> As he and his family sat around their meal that evening, Eustace was recounting his adventure of the morning. He got as far as '- so this fellow across the passage, he says, "Good morning, Eskimo",

and everybody burst out laughing.'

'But,' said his wife, 'what was so funny about that?'

Eustace pondered the matter long and earnestly. 'You know now that you ask I just can't see what's so funny about it. But, believe me, it sounded terribly funny at the time.'

The first thing I should say about this story is that the original exchange in the bus represented a good example of the kind of quick-fire pun that can be terribly funny. Not that there is anything so very funny in the confusion between the man from the Baltic and the man who lands on the lady's knee. That, if you like, is just one of Fowler's 'feeble puns'. No, it's not the pun itself but the speed and spontaneity with which it is produced that rightly guarantees it an immediate and hearty response. I might even be prepared to join issue with Fowler in his defence of puns *per se* and argue that all puns could fairly be called feeble puns but that the way in which a pun is produced can render it nothing short of scintillating. It wasn't the pun that sparkled. The brilliance lay not in the stone but in the setting.

I remember an occasion a good many years ago when an issue had arisen in high places in the Kirk regarding its traditional crest, a represenation of Moses' burning bush with the words *Nec Tamen Consumebatur* (nor was it ever consumed). Many loved traditions owe their existence to some chance, and so it is here for this whole affair began with an 'ornament' which a printer used to fill a blank space at the foot of a page. So the emblem came to be in popular use but has never been officially registered as a coat of arms with the Lyon King of Arms. Some of us felt we should go on using the crest as we had been doing for so many years. The Lord Lyon, on the other hand, was most insistent that we ought to register.

A meeting was held at which the Kirk was represented by the Principal Clerk and myself. It was pointed out to us that as things stood no one could interfere with our use of the crest, but that it would be easy for some institution or individual to adopt the badge, register it as their own and then interdict us from further use of it. 'For example, suppose a publican in the High Street were to hang a placard with a burning bush outside his door and register that as his official insignia there would be an end of the matter so far as the Kirk was concerned!' So warned the voice of officialdom. 'But,' I countered, 'a publican would never dream of using that emblem, for it is well known that good wine needs no bush burning or otherwise.' And James Longmuir did considerably better – said he, 'And it would be a mighty poor advert for anyone's beer to say it was never consumed.'

Not for a moment do I suggest that these were masterpieces of humour, but I do say they were neat in their context and, as with Eustace, they sounded very funny at the time. I find the very business of writing this down takes away from its effect. What depends almost wholly upon spontaneity must lose greatly when reduced to cold print.

To return, however, to Eustace the Laplander. The whole force of that joke – what lends it its quality of the ridiculous – is the man's inability to reproduce accurately at the dinner table the original pun perpetrated on the bus, producing Eskimo in place of Laplander.

The story illustrates a remarkably common phenomenon – the person who can never remember a joke. How often does one hear that phrase. I have no accurate statistical evidence but I should guess that nearly half the population will assure you that they suffer from this inability. What's more, they will usually record the fact as though they were registering some special virtue. To me it seems that the person claiming to suffer from this infirmity is suffering not from a defective memory but from a defective sense of humour, that is not primarily from an inability to remember the joke but from a failure to grasp the joke. It's not that the joke registered and was subsequently scrubbed from the memory tape; it is that it never truly registered on the tape at all. So that when such a person tries to retell the joke he is faced with the problem not of recreating a piece of humour but of reproducing a word-form. Had Friend Eustace really got the hang of the joke about Laplander he would never have forgotten it – what was there, after all, to remember? For him, it was just a collection of words that he tried to remember by rote – and for such learning he had little skill.

One evening in London, in a fairly large company, I heard a story of two men who had enjoyed a most successful night on the town. Some days later they met and one had a rueful story to tell of how just after their parting he had been picked up by the police and had spent the night in a cell. 'My, but you were lucky,' said his friend. 'I got home.' The story was well told and the company erupted. By an odd coincidence I was present a few days later in a different company when one of the party from the earlier gathering retold the story. He missed out the line about 'you were lucky', stating simply, 'O did you? I got home.' Needless to say, his hearers were waiting expectantly for the point of the joke so that they could laugh. I'm sure my friend wondered what had gone wrong and, like Eustace, would have claimed that 'it sounded very funny at the time.' I might add that the man in question is a distinguished actor who is in the way of playing humorous roles on the TV. I wonder whether he always understands completely the messages he so convincingly puts across.

A minister friend of mine who is no born comedian treasures as his *pièce de resistance* the following tortuous tale.

> A priest and a rabbi were neighbours at a large and flashy dinner party. Said the priest at one point, 'I'm going to have a second helping of this ham, it's so lovely and tender.' Only then did he notice the virgin condition of his neighbour's plate, which led him to ask, 'Aren't you having some, it's very tasty?' The Jew not unnaturally replied, 'I thought you would have known, my religion does not permit me to eat ham.' 'What a pity,' rejoined the priest, 'take it from me, it was delicious.'
>
> The evening's celebrations over, they were bidding one another goodnight. Said the rabbi, 'And do give my regards to your wife.'
>
> 'I thought you would have known,' rejoined the priest, 'my religion does not permit me to have a wife.'
>
> To which the Jew retorted, 'What a pity. Take it from me, they're delicious.'

Not in my opinion the funniest of stories. Least of all when you've heard it a few times. But to hear my friend tell it, it can be quite entertaining, for he often contrives to get the lines fankled, producing such results as advice to the rabbi to have a bit more wife, or the assurance that wives can be very tender. You find yourself listening with fascination to hear just how it's going to end up this time.

The perfect example, though, of the man who muffed his lines is this one about the shy young curate.

The shy young curate was greatly intrigued at a gathering one day to come across a colleague who appeared to find the business of meeting with strangers as easy and enjoyable as he for his part found it difficult and painful. He asked his new-found friend the secret of his masterly approach. 'There's really nothing to it,' the expansive one explained. 'it's just a matter of sizing up your victim and deciding on the best line of attack. One gambit which rarely fails is to start off with a little joke. Nothing elaborate,you understand, but a laugh can usually be counted on to slacken things up and before you know where you are you're getting along like life-long friends.'

'I met a chap just now who appeared a bit overpowering, so I said to him, "O, by the way, have you heard the story about the house with the dirty window?" When he said he hadn't I said, "There's really no use my telling it for you couldn't see through it." We positively sailed on from there.'

Some days later the shy young curate found himself sharing a sofa with a particularly frigid elderly lady upon whom his most profound observations on the state of religion were having as little effect as his most light-hearted comments about the weather. He remembered the joke technique. 'I wonder,' he enquired, 'whether you – er – ever heard the story about the house with the window you couldn't see through?' 'No,' she conceded, 'I can't say I have.'

'On second thoughts,' he said with a merry giggle, 'I don't think I should tell it to you. You see, it's too dirty.'

As I say he's probably still wondering why it proved so ineffective on his telling – it had sounded so good with the other chap.

For a pun to be funny it need not even have been intended by the perpetrator – often indeed the best of the joke lies in its having been accidental. There are times when it takes the hearer to take up the pun, the speaker having been in simple earnest in his use of the term. I'm especially fond of this yarn from a railway station of yester-year – in a day when trains had steam engines to pull them, when there were wee stations for them to stop at and when there were porters to open the doors when you got there.

Only a few minutes earlier, the local passenger train had stopped at the village station, where a couple of passengers had got on and three had got off and the guard had handed to the young porter a much-wrapped parcel. The train had steamed away, leaving the porter in sole possession of the platform – but with his parcel. His curiosity was whetted, for it was clear that a living creature was involved. So undoing the knot he prized open the lid just far enough to let him keek inside. What he saw was a little pup scratching and struggling for freedom. In fact its last struggle proved enough to knock the box out of the boy's hands and, as it fell on to the platform the puppy was able to effect its escape. Along the platform it scampered and up the stairs towards the street – hotly pursued, of course, by the porter.

As the pair emerged on to the roadway, the puppy continued its mad stampede and the boy was relieved to see a friend approaching along the road. 'Wullie,' he shouted, 'catch haud o' that dug – it's a parcel.'

Let's move to a new scene – to a University – to a history exam where the candidate referred to Bismark as 'the stormy petrol of Europe'. The examiner's marginal comment, 'Hail to thee, blithe spirit.' Or the candidate who insisted on siting the League of Nations at 'The Haig' to be advised, 'Don't be Vaig, ask for Hague.'

A pun may be effected by a play upon the different significance which a term enjoys when understood literally and that given in some figurative usage. There's the lovely tale of the two women who were discussing Church affairs and the one remarked she was sorry to see that 'oor minister's gettin' to be a richt auld man,' to which her friend responded, 'You're lucky – oors is gettin' to be a richt auld wife.'

The following story may appear too complicated to rest upon a simple pun, but it must be granted that the foundation is nothing more than a 'feeble pun'. A great deal of the power of the joke lies in the fact that you don't see it coming – indeed you may have to look for it after it has gone – and it's a good thing in any joke that it should leave something to be supplied by the hearer.Besides which, of course, it's a lovely tale of simple folk and a forgotten way of life.

The busy city magnate was worrying about his parents, for they were getting on in years and lived in glorious isolation in a cottage at the head of a Highland glen. Up till now he had been able to visit them with some regularity in the course of his far-reaching business trips. But he had got promotion, and while still having plenty of business trips these would mainly be taking him abroad. He talked the old couple into having the phone installed so he could keep in touch. They were not easy to persuade, for they were highly suspicious of such new-fangled contraptions, believing that if God in His inscrutable wisdom had intended we should use such devices He would certainly have arranged for us to be born suitably wired up.

Not many days later Donald and Maggie were preparing for bed when the phone rang. Apprehensively they looked one at the other.This was the moment they had been dreading. Said the Better Half, 'Tonald, you had better see to that.' Bracing himself for the ordeal Donald set off for the hall while Maggie listened from behind the bedroom door. 'Hello, hello,' she heard her husband saying. There was a considerable pause and then he continued, 'Yes, it is that, indeed and it is.' The phone was restored to its cradle and Donald returned to the bedroom.

'And whateffer was that all about?' anxiously enquired Maggie. 'I do not rightly understand,' explained Donald, 'but after I had called "Hello" someone came on the line and said, "It's a long distance from New York".'

That story, as I hinted, represents a fair bit of elaboration added to the basic pun. An even greater degree of elaboration is probably involved in this delightful tale from a school somewhere deep in the country.

The teacher had been explaining to her class that not always do we turn the singular into the plural by simply adding an 's'. She gave examples of man becomes men, foot becomes feet, ox becomes oxen, child becomes children, and so on. She ended up with a little test, going round the class giving the plural form of some word and expecting the child to come up with the singular. All went well till she confronted Charlie with the challenge of 'geese'. After only a moment's thought Charlie produced 'gimme'. No doubt at home he was accustomed indiscriminately to use 'Gimme a cup o' tea' or 'geese another slice o' bread'.

To return in closing to the simple type of pun that depends wholly on sharpness and speed and constitutes what could be called a 'smart crack'. This is a branch of the subject in which the person proposing to indulge in public speaking on platforms unprotected against hecklers would be well advised to become adept. What is needed always in that scene is not to convince the interrupter – on the unlikely assumption that he is capable of being convinced – but to silence him. And for that two things are essential, a quick tongue and a rapier-sharp wit. An audience may enjoy the cheeky intervention; they will relish still more hearing the interrupter bested at his own game.

That type of humour, though, does not retell very well. It is very much an affair of the occasion, depending for its effect on the atmosphere and the general environment. Here, quite accurately is the kind of humour which 'sounded terribly funny at the time' but which can be a bit flat when retold. One solitary example illustrates why one is enough.

The political speaker was putting the rhetorical question,'What is crippling this nation today?' 'Is it Socialism?' he asked. 'Or is it Capitalism?' A voice from the back of the hall suggested helpfully, 'Naw, ye eediot, it's rheumatism.'

I cannot leave the subject of the pun without recounting a remark I heard on the radio a few years ago. I am almost certain that the pun was not deliberate and that indeed the speaker did not properly appreciate what he had said. For his own subsequent peace of mind I can only hope that was so. I cannot remember what was the subject under discussion, all I recall was the description of some particular aspect of it as a 'virgin field pregnant with possibilities.'

If we can have a mixed metaphor why not a mixed pun?

CHAPTER TWO

THE SIXTH SENSE

THE FIRST CHAPTER OPENED with an attempt to answer the question, 'What is a joke?' It might be an idea to open this chapter with the question, 'What is a sense of humour?'

In the previous chapter I talked about the number of people who claim inability to remember a joke. Distinctly worse are those who are constitutionally incapable of seeing a joke – though they, oddly enough, are not so proud of their infirmity as are the amnesia brigade. They may laugh appreciatively with other members of the company when humour is in the air, so to speak, but they haven't a clue as to what it's all about. Not infrequently they are quite good at remembering and retelling jokes and can be popular after-dinner speakers but they suffer from a deficient sense of humour none the less.

Many people have a quick eye for what is funny but are utterly devoid of a sense of humour. They will laugh – right heartily – at situations of the slapstick variety; they will never tire of seeing custard puddings projected into human faces; they will go into paroxysms at the spectacle of a man passing through a door and, in so doing, emptying a bucket of water over himself. But that is neither more nor less than clowning and, while it may belong to the family of humour, it is, in my view, a poor relation of that family.

An appreciation of fun is something totally different from a sense of humour – you need only eyes to see fun; you must have a sense of humour to see a joke.

The essential point about true humour – as opposed to fun – is that the recipient has to make his contribution if the joke is to achieve fulfilment. Thus a man with what we call a keen sense of humour will find amusement in situations that leave others stone cold. On the other side, the man who is without a sense of humour will never get round to seeing the point in even the most laughable of situations.

What is a sense of humour? It is, as the name suggests, one of the senses, a sixth sense surely, and for that reason falls into a special category. How would you begin to define a sense of touch, smell, or hearing? For the person who has it, no definition is necessary, for the person who doesn't have it, no amount of defining will help. A sense of humour is something that enables us to detect the presence of the amusing and the ridiculous. Let us feel deeply grateful if we have it and profoundly sympathetic towards those who have not.

Harken to this little tale.

The young man had come home for a holiday after a spell of farming in one of the more remote regions of Africa. He was being asked about conditions, prices, wages and what have you. Do you get much rain? asked one of the company. 'We had about eight inches last year.' was the reply. 'Just eight inches – that's not a lot of rain,' contributed another. 'Maybe not,' said the farmer, 'but you wouldn't be saying that if you had been there the night it fell.'

I venture to think you will find that little exchange mildly amusing or just plain stupid according to whether or not you are equipped with a sense of humour.

In this same connection the following comparative study is not without interest, even if it suffers from all the horrors that flow from generalisation.

It is said that the average Englishman laughs three times over the one joke – out of politeness when you tell it to him, later when you explain it to him and a third time when the penny drops and he sees what it had all been about. You may be itching to tell me that you have never known this to happen and I am itching to reply that I have never met the average Englishman.

The average Welshman laughs only twice, first out of politeness and then out of enjoyment when you expound to him the point of the tale.

The average Irishman laughs only once because he sees it while you are in process of telling it.

The average Scot, on the other hand, does not laugh at all because he heard the joke years ago and he doesn't think it all that funny anyway.

Now, I'd be the first to admit that this kind of thing is highly misleading and may even be defamatory. It's nonsense to allocate the ability to see a joke on a nationalistic basis, but there are three things that can still be said in its defence. First, the story speaks about the average Englishman without telling us where that person is to be found or how identified. I've certainly still to meet the average Scot. As one might say if we were still in the chapter on puns, it's real mean to talk about a mean without first telling us what you mean. Second, you do come across individuals of whatever nationality who conform to one of the four types. And third, there are easily identifiable traits in humour as in other qualities but, that apart, there is a vast difference in the reaction to a particular joke between for example the Scot and his southern neighbour. I have attended meetings in the metropolis at which people have been literally rolling in the aisles at some pun which in my view deserved a raspberry, and then later some salty observation of a really clever kind was allowed to pass unheeded because, presumably, it was too subtle to have been recognised as a deliberate sally.

Let me quote a specific instance of the slowness to pick up what I consider a pretty obvious joke. In the course of quite a bit of after-dinner speaking I am on occasion invited either to propose or to reply to the toast of the Guests. This is not always the easiest of assignments, and I rather like the following story, which has some obvious relevance to the subject.

As a young man I used to spend the occasional holiday in the house of a shepherd in the heart of Galloway's hills. Quite nearby was a tinkers' encampment and quite often I would wander across for a crack – always worth the walk. . .

One evening I found the usual fire blazing and, stripped to the waist, a massive tinker holding his shirt over the fire just clear of the flames. 'My goodness, Jock,' I said, 'what in the world are you doing there?'

'I'm toasting the guests,' was the laconic reply.

Not infrequently I find I have to make a deliberate and over-elaborate pause at the end of that tale to indicate that the whole story has now been told and that, accordingly, peals of laughter will be appreciated. Even when the response has been fairly spontaneous I have noticed that the laughter comes on, as it were, in waves (sometimes just in ripples) as one group after another gets round to seeing the point.

I had, however, what I can only describe as a disastrous experience with that story at a function one evening in London when perhaps half a dozen of the diners laughed while the hundreds looked round mystified, clearly wondering what, if anything there was to laugh at.

Meanwhile, the joke disappeared without trace. Some of them may well have seen the point of it the next day but that was little comfort to me. For all that, according to my reckoning it's a remarkably good joke – all the better for not being too obvious.

In the realm of the single-sentence joke which, if you're not on your toes, can pass before you've seen it, there's none I prefer to the tale of the jeweller who displayed in his shop window a notice which read 'Ears Pierced While You Wait'. Not infrequently – even after a long pause to let the message sink in – I've had to go on and add, 'But he didn't say what was the alternative to waiting.' It then becomes a case of 'Jokes Explained While You Wait', or 'Dense Heads Pierced Along With Ears – No Extra Charge.' And that is never a very satisfactory state of affairs. A joke may gain in the telling – it can only lose in the explaining.

Sometimes I think it's a mistake even to begin to explain a joke. If it hasn't had an instant appeal it has failed as a joke and there is nothing you can subsequently do that will save it – you can hold a post mortem on it, but you cannot give it the kiss of life. If on Guy Fawkes Night one of your squibs doesn't go off at the first time of asking you will be well advised to throw it into the nearest pond. In no circumstances should you tinker with it in the hope of making it work, for almost certainly it will blow up in your face. The same is true, I am sure, of the joke that doesn't go off at the first time of telling. Abandon it. Write it off. Pretend you had just been speaking to yourself. Even admit it must be your fault – you must have got the story wrong. But don't try to explode it by artifice. Only trouble can result from that.

It must, I feel sure, be a terrifying experience to be left with an unexploded bomb in your hands; it is, I can vouch from experience, a most humiliating experience to be left with an unexploded joke on your lips.

Which raises the question as to how you get out of a situation like that. It's tempting to try another joke, but the chances are that you'll fare no better with that. Instead you may well be deeper in the mire.

Readily I will grant you that there are jokes of so pawky a character as to appeal primarily if not exclusively to the Scot. Doubtless examples of other types of humour are equally endemic to other climes. It would not surprise me, for instance, if only a limited number of people could find anything funny in the following homely little yarn. I shouldn't blame those who admit they can't. But I'd be sorry for them, for they are definitely missing something. And yet, let's be frank, I'm hanged if I know how I'd begin to explain the point of the joke – if joke it is.

The door on the tenement stairhead was opened fractionally by a small boy.

'Is your father in?' enquired the visitor.

'Naw,' said the boy with a shake of the head as he was about to shut the door.

'When are you expectin' him back?' persisted the visitor.

'We're no' expectin' him back,' said the boy with some finality – 'he died last Tuesday.' Again he was about to close the door as firmly as he had closed the conversation.

But the visitor was not to be put off. 'He didna say onything aboot a wee pot o' yella paint afore he died, did he?'

As I say, national differences of outlook and temperament can go far to explain why what is deadly serious to one can be outrageously funny to another. The following incident, which actually occurred, makes the point admirably.

The tourist from the States had been having a wonderful time in Glasgow unearthing information about her forbears and even discovering the burial place of some of them in the Necropolis. It was natural, therefore, that on the Sunday morning she should attend service in the Cathedral. She was chatting afterwards with a fellow-worshipper. 'That,' she affirmed, 'was a deeply mooven eggsperience – most deeply mooven.' Her new-found companion – Glasgow native – conceded it might have been worse. She persisted: 'Why does the preacher wear that rad cassock under his gown?' That, it was explained, was the mark of a royal chaplain – when a minister was invited to join Her Majesty's Ecclesiastical Household in Scotland he earned the right to wear a red cassock.

'You mean,' said Uncle Sam's niece in hushed and reverend tones, 'that minister actually preaches before Her Majesty?' It was agreed he had doubtless done so from time to time.

'Ya know,' drawled the reply, 'that makes the eggsperience all the more deeply mooven.'

As an example from the other side of the coin – the American enjoyment of humour when we can detect little – I might tell this yarn which had gained vast popularity around Chicago some years ago. In its way it's quite an entertaining picture that's painted, and there's a neat little moral to it, but as a cannie Scot I couldn't imagine myself going head over heels in the enjoyment of it as a joke, as so many of my Yankee friends were doing.

Buster's offer of a lift had been blithely accepted by his friend Hank. They were chatting happily as they drove along when, to Hank's alarm, they crashed unconcernedly through traffic lights set clearly at red. 'Gosh,' spluttered Hank, 'did you not see these lights were at red?' 'Sure,' replied Buster, 'I saw them but I didn't bother. My brother does that all the time.' Hank was not reassured.

Not many crossings later the incident was repeated to the accompaniment of screeching brakes and blaring horns from law-abiding citizens. 'I tell you,' said Buster, 'that's how my brother tells me you ought to drive – he never drives any other way.'

By this time Hank was wishing he had declined the offer of the lift and then, to his intense surprise, his friend drew to a halt at lights which were at green in his favour. 'Why are you stopping here?' Hank enquired.

'Well,' drawled Buster, 'it just dawned on me that my brother might be coming on the other road.'

Some would not think that funny at all; some might even think it pathetic; but I tell you I have seen a whole company convulsed at the hearing of it.

This might be as good a place as any for me to squeeze in a couple of jokes about the same subject, with many points of similarity, but utterly different in every important respect. Let the stories speak for themselves. The former might carry the title 'Revenge is Sweet'.

Rehearsals for the primary school Nativity Play were thrown into confusion when the six-year old boy cast as Joseph was struck down with a chill that kept him at home for a week. Some hasty reshuffling was undertaken with the result that when Joseph returned he discovered that, though widely recognised as the finest actor of his year, he had lost the star role, being awarded instead that of the Innkeeper, an absolutely worthless part requiring only that he appear at a door, shake his head, shrug his shoulders, spread out his hands and generally make it clear that the Virgin and her husband had better seek digs elsewhere.

As was to be expected of any artist in such circumstances Joseph-turned-Innkeeper smarted under this terrible affront. Though probably it didn't occur to him in these terms, it was as though Laurence Olivier had been relegated from the part of Macbeth to that of the Second Murderer. Rehearsals with the rearranged cast, however, proceeded smoothly and without hitch.

On the day of the performance, with adoring parents packed into the school hall, moist-eyed and clutching their handkerchiefs, Joseph-turned-Innkeeper exacted his terrible revenge.

As Joseph, his five-year old travel-weary bride at his side, trudged heavily up to the Inn and knocked on the door showing he knew his quest to be a hopeless one, the Innkeeper sprang out, beaming expansively and in a clear welcoming voice proclaimed, 'But of course, come right through, there's plenty of room in the inn.'

A suitable name for the latter would be 'It's Compassion that Counts.'

Some difficulty had been experienced in the country school over the casting of the Nativity Play. In particular the problem centred around the position of Willie. Now, as everybody knew, Willie was endowed with less than average intelligence, but he was far and away the most generous, kindly and lovable boy in the school. He was absolutely set on being given a part and nobody had the heart to say him nay. It was decided to make him Innkeeper. All he had to do in that role was to appear at the door, shake his head and say, 'Sorry there isn't a room, not a single room,' and shut the door. Not even Willie could contrive to muff these lines and at rehearsal all went splendidly.

Came the night of the performance and all was proceeding according to plan. The woebegone couple appeared at the Inn and Joseph told of their plight. 'Sorry there isn't a room,' said Willie the Innkeeper – and then the true Willie broke out through the make-up, 'But och, come awa' ben, ye can have my room.'

As I say, how alike yet how utterly different.

Since we've got back to the country and simple folk, how about this as an example of the joke painting a homely but amusing picture.

The minister, while able to take the funeral service in the house of sorrow, had a previous engagement that prevented his going to the committal. So he spoke to one of his elders who, he insisted, could perfectly well conduct the short service at the graveside. The elder showed a distinct lack of enthusiasm, but after a bit of cajoling agreed that if suitable words of committal were written down in large and legible hand, he would be prepared to read it. The text was duly delivered and carefully pasted into the crown of the deputy's lum hat.

At the place of interment, the elder solemnly took up his stance at the head of the open grave and, as the coffin was being lowered took off his hat and, with great deliberation, began, 'Let us pray. O Lord, this is no' my hat!'

It's a fairly natural transition from the wrong hat to the wrong documents. How's this for a muddle.

It was during the war and the soldier, who had been granted some kind of compassionate leave to allow of his getting wed, was moving north on the night train.

All the formalities of proclamation, procuring of marriage certificate etc had been completed and he had the papers to prove it in his great-coat pocket. He was snuggled up in a corner of a compartment managing to catch a blink when, somewhere around Leeds, he was rudely awakened by a ticket collector who shook him by the shoulder and demanded to see his ticket. Still only half awake the poor chap fumbled in his great-coat pocket and handed over not the ticket but the wedding papers.

'O yes,' said the railway official after due inspection, 'These will take you a long weary journey – but not on British Rail.'

It is universally accepted that one man's meat is another man's poison – at least it is accepted in theory. But when it comes to practice we're slow to recognise the implications of the principle. How many of the miscalculations we make in life arise from our failure to appreciate the truth of this dictum? For, whatever we may profess to the contrary, our tendency is to imagine that in any given situation the reaction of the normally intelligent citizen will be identical to our own. Each of us is convinced that he represents a fair sample of homo sapiens. It may be that we are right in this, but it does not follow that one fair sample in any way resembles another fair sample. The thing that would be anathema to me might represent the height of someone else's ambition; my dream could be my neighbour's nightmare. The kind of situation that can arise when we are taken completely by surprise by the attitude of our neighbour can form the basis of a joke. This little anecdote makes the point with admirable force.

The man who presented himself at the office of the Registrar of Births, Marriages and Deaths was most anxious to learn whether there was any way he could change his name. The Registrar told him it was quite possible but it involved a fairly complicated procedure known as Deed Poll. It was a thing he wouldn't recommend, but in exceptional circumstances it could be invoked. 'What,' he asked, 'is your name?' The visitor hung his head in shame. 'Charlie Stink,' he muttered in tones scarcely audible across the counter.

'Well, yes,' the Registrar said, a new note of sympathy creeping into his voice, 'I can quite see the point. Yes, yes, if you will just take a seat for a few minutes I will get the necessary papers and we'll see what we can do for you.' Having returned with the appropriate forms and laboriously entered the particulars – full name, place and date of birth, parents' names, mother's maiden name, present address – he went on, 'What do you want to be called – what would you like to change your name to?'

With the happy smile of a man about to be released from the chains of an ancient bondage the applicant announced happily, 'Willie Stink.'

What lends that story its point as a joke is, of course, the jolt the hearer receives on learning that it is not the surname but the christian name that the man is so keen to have altered. A fair amount of humour consists in leading the hearer up the garden path. To me the interesting thing about this story is the point it is making – in however ludicrous a fashion – that what would be abhorrent to Everyman was of no particular concern to This Man. He was perfectly happy to be called Stink, but Charles he could not abide. As I have said, one man's poison is another man's fizzy drink.

It might be added that the choice of 'Willie' as the improvement on 'Charlie' introduces a neat little pun that is a significant bonus to an already good joke.

In the field of humour as in all departments of life this principle of one man's meat obtains, and you will find people who think the very acme of fun has been achieved in a joke which will leave others stone cold. The 'poison' aspect may on occasion be represented in the fact that there are those for whom a certain type of joke is worse than distasteful, positively poisonous. For example, I find the purely dirty joke and the suggestive pun utterly unentertaining. The other evening on the TV someone described a dog balanced on three legs at a lamp-post as The Leaning Pee-er of Tausa. I find it difficult to conceive of anything less funny than a concoction of that sort.

The trouble with this kind of joke is that the offence against good taste is treated as itself a form of humour. It's not even an acceptable substitute for humour. I don't see myself as all that mealy-mouthed, but for me a fair amount of what is put across on the media as entertainment of the first class would be hard pressed to merit a third class ticket. It will evoke a laugh, but listen carefully and you'll find it's an artificial, even hysterical kind of laughter. It's not an expression of enjoyment but a cover-up for embarrassment. What evidence I have leads me to think that it does not appeal to the population as a whole. And even if it did one is entitled to ask how far a public service has a responsibility to educate and uplift rather than to cater for the debased and the depraved.

My own impression has always been that suggestive humour represents the last deformity of witty minds. When we are no longer able to get new material we can always fall back on smut and be sure of a response. It's sad, in a way, to hear a comedian capable of putting across good clean fun reduced to the kind of stuff designed to set schoolboys sniggering in the privy.

Mark you, I'm not without sympathy for the professional comic of today. Time was when he could muster a programme of first-class material and put it across in the halls, a fortnight here, three weeks yonder, and it lasted him for years. Today he makes a single appearance 'on the box' and tomorrow his best cracks are old hat from Land's End to John o' Groats. Which leads me to ask an interesting question: whether a joke is any the less funny because you've heard it before. No small part of the success of a song lies in the quality of the singing, and not many of us would scorn a concert by a great vocalist because we were familiar with every item on his programme.

A predecessor of mine in the ministry of my first parish gained a great reputation as a speaker in a day when the *soirée* was an important feature of Church life. He had, it would seem, quite a repertoire, but, far more important, he had what was nothing short of a genius for story-telling. So much so, I believe, it was no unusual thing when he appeared on a platform for people to call out out, 'Tell us the one about the so-and-so.' That to me has always seemed to be the hall-mark of greatness in this field. Any member of the audience could have told the tale, they were all familiar with the denouement, but it was still worthwhile to hear him tell it.

To return, however, to my complaint about smut. I hope I may not be accused of saying that nothing represents good healthy fun that would not have been acceptable to a Victorian audience. All I am trying to say is that a joke is not outrageously funny because it would have been banned from a Victorian drawing-room. Given that the story is sufficiently funny of itself then a fair leeway may be allowed as against the standards of the drawing-room of the good Queen Vic. Is there anywhere in existence a picture of that lady convulsed in mirth? Even at that I think there is a real virtue for a comedian in setting clear boundaries to the distance he is prepared to travel in this direction.

Let me add a silly little pun – one that would certainly not have been welcomed in a Victorian day and indeed might have been frowned upon in some Elizabethan ones. It is attributed to the great Dr John White, minister for some years at Shettleston and twice Moderator of the Kirk's General Assembly.

For many years Dr White had been a member of Shettleston Parish Council, once a very important body but one whose functions had been gradually whittled away in a changing pattern of local government. The Parish Council had been relieved of responsibility for the poor, for education, for roads and sewers, and so on. One of the few duties remaining to it was that of providing, maintaining and generally being responsible for public toilet facilities, and this led Dr White to say that from a Parish Councillor he had been promoted to being a Privy Councillor.

And how about this one to close the chapter.

The after-lunch speaker had sent a last-minute apology to the Rotary Club, so that time looked like hanging heavy on their hands. The President reported what had happened and went on to say that he decided that the best plan would be for them all to put their names in a hat and whoever was drawn would occupy the available ten or fifteen minutes by giving a talk off the cuff on any subject of his own choosing. No one was madly enthusiastic about the plan but, in the absence of a better one they unanimously agreed.

When finally the 'winner' had been selected he not unnaturally regretted his rashness and wanted to call off. He was reminded, however, that a bargain was a bargain and that had someone else been drawn he would have been the first to expect the unlucky one to play the game. 'All right,' said he, 'I'll give you a talk. Just sit back and I'll give you a talk on "The Seamy Side of My Sex Life".'

The man had considerable gifts as a raconteur and either life had brought him into many strange situations or, more likely, he was equipped with a fertile imagination – at any rate he held his audience spellbound with his romantic adventures. His was universally acclaimed as the best after-dinner speech the club had ever enjoyed. Someone even wanted to propose a vote of thanks to the speaker who had failed to turn up!

Elated with so much unaccustomed praise the speaker was misguided enough on getting home to tell his wife about what had occurred – in not too much detail. 'A funny thing happened at the Rotary Club today,' he said and went on to explain about his name coming out of the hat and about what an overwhelming success he had proved. His wife, as is the custon of wives, was a little sceptical. 'Oh,' said her man reassuringly, 'I was great. Everyone said it was the best talk they had had in years.' Still she was unconvinced. 'What did you get to talk about anyway?' At this point, not surprisingly, his courage faltered and he replied, 'Yachting.'

'Yachting!' she exploded. 'What in all the world do you know about yachting?' He confessed that from the practical point of view he knew remarkably little about yachting, but went on to expound, 'It's not what you know about it that counts, it's the way you can put it across. It's just that some folk have a natural gift for public speaking, and that's what they all said about me.' The lady was still highly sceptical, but there the matter was allowed to rest.

It was some days later when she was out shopping that she ran into the President of the Club. 'Hello, Mrs Brown,' he greeted her, 'you never let on that your man was an after-dinner speaker cordon blue.' 'Ay,' said she, still highly sceptical, 'he was telling me about this carry-on you had the other day.'

'He was great, just great,' said the President. 'It was far and away the best speech we've had in years. And all straight off the cuff.'

'Well,' said the lady, yielding a little in her incredulity, 'maybe he was, but it beats me what he got to talk about, for he's only done it twice in his life. The first time he was sick; the second time his hat blew off.'

CHAPTER THREE

SURELY WORTH A SMILE

WHO MAKES UP ALL THESE JOKES ANYWAY? A question often
enough asked and one to which I'd dearly love to know the answer.
Of course, it presupposes knowledge of the answer to an earlier
question - how is a joke made up? It's easy to picture some solemn-
looking soul sitting by his guttering candle in the seclusion of some
attic making up a series of side-splitting puns and wise-cracks of
the word-joke variety. But the situation joke, I am inclined to
think, was like Topsy – not born but just growed – out of some
chance unrehearsed incident. How often have I found myself
saying of some gem of this type that it simply had to be genuine –
it was far too clever for anyone possibly to have thought it up!

This much is certain, that I cannot claim to be in any manner
a maker-up of jokes. I confess to having been guilty of a few puns
in my time (clever ones I like to think), and I would modestly
claim to have improved the quality of some stories I've heard others
retelling badly - but that's as far as I would go. What I can claim is
that I happen to suffer from a remarkably good memory in the
field of fun. Let me once hear a funny story and without any
deliberate act of will I can be counted upon to remember it, not for
days but for ever after. Not only so, I can normally recall from
whom I heard it and the circumstances in which it was told. How
I wish for a like ability to recall names and faces, and to remember
the errands I promised my wife I would perform.

Dr W M Macgregor, Principal of Trinity College, Glasgow's
Theological School, used to amaze his students by the way in
which, without the slightest scrap of notes, he could quote from
the whole field of literature, English, Classical, French. There he
would stand, chatting on some theme, and the references and the
quotations would simply flow, apparently without ending.

Someone once congratulated him on his good memory, to which Williemac (as he was affectionately known) replied, 'I don't have a good memory; I've got a shocking memory. I can't forget a single thing.' I think I can understand how he felt, and within the strictly limited - and, let it be said, remarkably useless - field of the funny story I can claim to enjoy a 'shocking memory'.

While, then, I could not even begin to invent, make up, think up, or whatever the proper term may be, a collection of jokes, it would subject my memory to no great strain to compile a collection of 'Jokes I Have Heard' or, if you prefer it, 'Jokes I Have Told.' They would be the same jokes, for in the domain of the after- dinner story the normal rules about plagiarism do not apply. They just couldn't be enforced. Certainly I would be hard pressed to prove it was my story, but you would have as big a job proving it had been yours.

It has in fact frequently been put to me that I should compile such a collection of funny stories, but it is a suggestion I have never felt any inclination to follow up. On the very odd occasion when I have written down a joke it has always seemed to me a particularly cold-blooded exercise, and I have found difficulty in identifying this dull, dead thing on the paper with the living, sparkling reality that had sent people into stitches. Humour, like good works, is a spontaneous affair that is desperately impoverished when it is made subject to premeditation and deliberation and becomes the subject of a vote For or Against. I've never found a collection of butterflies fixed to a card an especially inspiring spectacle. The thought of compiling a Bumper Book of Fun holds for me mighty little attraction.

It is alleged - and I can well believe it - that a farmer once said of ministers that they were like dung, they did an awfu' lot o' guid when they were weel spread oot through the country, but ye didna want to meet ower mony o' them thegither in the wan place. (It sounds as though he had been attending the Assembly.) The choice in fact is that between a fertiliser and a midden. It is an analogy I should not want to pursue too far, but the distinction is sound enough and, as I see it, can equally fairly be applied to the field of the humorous. The occasional apposite, neat little flash of wit can bring the whole speech to life while a solid mass of indifferent jokes can be, at the kindliest estimate, off-putting and wearisome.

I never cease to marvel at the after-dinner speaker who can stand rhyming joke after joke without there being any connection between the jokes themselves or any relation between any one of them and the theme of the toast. He is proud to have collected a number of new stories and he is determined to let the company have the benefit of them all, one after the other in rapid succession and, as I say, without rhyme or reason so far as the order of their telling is concerned and without any apparent reason why in the prevailing circumstances any of them should be told at all. To me one of the first requirements of a speech is that the speaker address himself to his theme and that his remarks follow a logical sequence – in a word that there should be some kind of bone-structure to his talk. If he can illustrate his contentions in an entertaining way with yarns that are relevant and to the point this is admirable and is the mark of true genius. He may even be permitted the odd digression to take in some pleasantry for its own sake, though this should be done sparingly. Who is to know – or to care – if some of the contentions owe their presence to the fact that they can be illustrated by a good story he's itching to tell. But, like the ministers and the manure, the stories should be 'weel spread oot'.

What applies to a speech would seem to apply no less forcibly to a book, so if I were contemplating producing a compendium of funny stories it would have to be of such a kind that the tales were not thrown together in some massive pile but would appear in an intelligible sequence so that each at least gave the impression of having a justification for its appearance where it was. Let there be some reasonable framework to hold the whole affair together – a recognisable element of bone-structure.

It occurred to me that if one were hell-bent on producing some sort of work on the subject of merriment an anatomy was much to be preferred to any type of anthology. Here one could try to set things into a recognisable order and at the same time to disclose the reason for that order. Here one could try in a modest way to classify and arrange and systematise and categorise. An Anatomy of Mirth seemed to offer real attractions. In the following pages, then, I have sought not merely to record some of the amusing stories, the clever wise-cracks, the entertaining situations that I have come across in the course of the years, but I've tried also to set them forth in a coherent and logical order and, more ambitious still, I have attempted an explanation of what it is that makes a joke tick, why a particular situation should prove mirth-provoking. This might be described as an essay in analysing bone-structure – so why not call it an anatomy?

It is, I suppose, inevitable that a fair proportion of the stories with which I am most familiar should be of Scottish extraction and should properly be told in the doric. This presents an acute problem. It is always possible to translate the material into good copy-book English, the trouble being that a tale doesn't seem right in that kind of garb and, what is worse, the joke usually contrives to get lost in the changing-room. The obvious alternative is to transliterate. But this is never easy and if carried too far can render the material unintelligible to many readers. I have tried to steer a middle course, using Scottish terms wherever these are appropriate while in the case of words common to both languages I have interfered with the spelling as little as possible – just enough, I hope, to indicate that a BBC accent would be quite out of place. The Scottish reader will, I trust, experience little difficulty. For others, I have tried to adhere fairly closely to normal spellings.

It goes without saying that the same difficulty obtains in the case of Gaels from the far islands, in the case of tourists from the far Americas, in the case of quite a bit of Glasgow's population from far Pakistan – and so on. As best I could I have tried to indicate the general lines of the accents used, because without capturing something of the vital character of the occasion you will never get the flavour of the story. In every case, though, I must be dependent upon the sympathetic reader to supply what at best I can indicate only very sketchily by means of transliteration.

I have something to say later about national characteristics in the field of humour. But different reactions to the humorous are not to be found only as between one nation and another, there are wide divergences between various classes of people within the one nation – within the one city, if it comes to that. I think, for example, of how different the humour of Glasgow can be from that of the Scottish countryside, and of how the latter itself varies according to whether you are in the south-west, or in the north-east, or in any of the regions between.

There is something rather obvious (and very cheeky) about the city laugh – as in the claim that a photographer went to take a picture of plumbers at work, but one of them moved and spoiled it. The ideal humourist in the countryman's book is the man who can 'slip them in awfu' cautious', the type of humour commonly described as 'pawky', the sort of thing you can miss if you're not listening carefully – and don't imagine your host is going to help – he's far too much of a gentleman to draw attention to the fact that your slip is showing.

Deliberately the witticism is worked in with misleading solemnity. I remember an old lady in Fife saying of her new minister (whose preaching apparently lacked body) that it was 'like asking you to draw in yer chair to an oot fire.' My one-time parish of Houston was served by a railway station two miles from the village. A native, asked the stupid question why the station was so far away replied that he supposed (*sic*) that it was to have it beside the railway.

In what follows I have tried to draw upon the resources of both town and country, but if one is to appreciate the true flavour of either one has to have a consciousness of the total difference of approach.

In concluding these preliminary observations let me say that I do not expect that all who read the subsequent pages will find the arguments convincing or even find the jokes amusing, though I hope they may be rewarded with a smile. One of the most baffling aspects of this subject of humour is audience reaction. How is it that what sets one gathering in stitches sets another if not in tears at least gey near it, why is it that in some companies you'll get a laugh every time you pause for breath while in others you'll not elicit so much as a titter when you've reached the culmination of what you thought was your best joke, why does the mere sight of one audience inspire you while the very appearance of another is enough to grind you into the dust? An explanation there must be for a phenomenon so striking.

It's tempting to say the whole thing depends upon atmosphere, the shape of the hall, how the audience is seated relative to the speaker and to one another, the comparative size of the gathering, whether it had been a good meal, the nature of the occasion, and so on. Now it is perfectly true that all of these factors play their part – an important part at that. Sometimes you'll speak at a function where the diners are spread through a series of small rooms so that in no way can you see your audience – and that's a big handicap before you've even got to your feet. Again – increasingly commonly – a dinner may be held in a function room which has as its centre a small square of polished floor where the dancing is to take place and with the tables occupying the carpeted area all around. The result is that the speaker has immediately in front of him the empty space constituting the dance floor surrounded by a fringe audience. The poor chap is not inspired in the least to be talking at so much highly polished wood, and the audience is constantly reminded of the pleasure awaiting them if only he would dry up – which is never a big help. A company of fewer than say forty can be surprisingly difficult to address in an entertaining way. You might think there would be a warm, friendly, homely feeling that would make speech-making easy, but this in fact is not so. The speech that would go high in a crowded hall just does not come off in the comparative intimacy of a small group seated around one table. Better really to sit and chat to them, but that is quite a different technique. Then, as must be obvious, if the company has been indifferently dined they will not be in the most receptive frame of mind for an address, no matter how entertaining. And – what can be still more trying – if the company has been too successfully wined they will not be sure whether to guffaw or to fall asleep. They may even get around to interrupting by way of lending a hand. O yes, there are many things to militate against the efforts of the would-be wit.

Even accepting all that – and I'm sure it's all desperately important – one has still not explained completely this phenomenon of the differing responses of differing audiences. I had the point forcibly brought home to me some years ago. As a minister I have had not a little experience of proposing the health of the happy couple after a wedding reception dinner. It happened on one occasion that I had two of these affairs on consecutive evenings. They were held in the same hostelry, the number of guests was substantially equal, we were even treated to the identical meal. The couples, I should say, belonged to essentially the same social stratum, and the one set of guests looked remarkably like the other. In short the second reception was, to all appearing, an exact replica of the first.

I had a fairly carefully prepared speech on the Tuesday evening and it was very well received, every subtlest innuendo was picked up and the more obvious cracks brought howls of appreciation. So, not unnaturally, I repeated the performance on the Wednesday. This time it fell flat on its face. My best jokes were hard put to it to elicit a smile. Clearly here was a case where other things were all equal, so how to explain so completely different a reception for the identical speech? In the end I imagine we have just to fall back on the doctrine that while a joke may be quite funny in its own limited sphere there is in the last analysis nothing quite so funny as folk.

CHAPTER FOUR

NEAR THE BONE

THERE IS A MOST INTERESTING field of humour where what earns the laugh is not any enormously – or even mildly – funny situation but simply the fact that the whole thing comes so close to the truth – that it cuts so near to the bone. The resulting sharp tang of cynicism is what lends relish to the dish. Take that away and you've nothing left. The joke, therefore, may well be tied to a particular period in time or even to a specific incident in history, since it is within that context alone that the cynical element gains its relevance. You might call it 'situation-humour'.

To take a simple instance there's the story, very meaningful today, that might be entitled 'Cottage Pie in Darkest Africa'.

Two cannibals in a corner of the African jungle were standing at the side of a large goblet of missionary broth which one of them was stirring assiduously as it simmered on a great fire. Pausing in his efforts for long enough to sip some of the brew he smacked his lips – 'Great stuff,' he opined, 'lovely flavour.' His friend, with relish as obvious as it was audible, was gnawing at a bone. 'I tell you what it is,' he responded, 'this is a damn sight better than yon cottage pie they served up to us in the canteen at the London School of Economics.'

There's nothing really funny in that tale. On the contrary it is distinctly sad in its implication that the veneer of civilisation acquired by attendance at a British institution can be so wafer thin. But that, of course, is the whole point of the story. You might call it a sick joke, but I would not myself subscribe to that view. To me it's just a joke that's gey near the bone.

Not surprisingly, perhaps, there is a wealth of jokes of this type connected with the Kirk, in particular with people's attitude to the responsibilities and with their response to its demands. The following may be quite a joke, but I can testify that it has also the distinction of being literally true.

> The only reason the mother who was completely unconnected with the congregation could advance in support of her request for the minister to baptise her fourth child was, 'Weel, it was you that 'did' the ither three.' 'But surely,' remonstrated the minister, 'the fact that I allowed myself to be persuaded against my better judgment three times in the past is no reason why I should go on doing so for ever.'
>
> 'At least,' said the lady with some show of reason, 'ye canna say I ever gaed by ye.'

For the literal accuracy of this companion-tale I am not prepared to vouch, but I would affirm that if not true it surely ought to be, for it so perfectly characterises both a type and an attitude. Time and again I've come across this kind of thing if never so neatly or so humorously portrayed. I suppose you could call it 'One Good Turn Deserves Another'.

> ✓ The farmer had called at the manse to seek baptism for his bairn. Under examination he freely admitted that he was not a member of the Church, neither was his wife, they never came to Church, they didn't subscribe to the Church, it was not their intention to mend their ways. But he wanted 'the wean done,' and he was obviously at a loss to understand the reluctance of the minister to comply.
>
> The minister went on to pose the reasonable enough question, 'Since, then, you have nothing whatever to do with my Church why should you come and ask me to baptise your infant?' 'It's like this,' said the farmer, 'ye bocht twa cairt o' dung frae me in the spring o' the year an' I thocht I wad like to gi'e ye a bit turn.'

On one occasion I had a most unusual reason put to me as to why I should conduct a marriage.

> ✓ I was an Assistant at the time and my minister being on holiday I was standing in at the vestry hour. A middle-aged couple was shown in. The woman's face was familiar and I recalled that about twelve months before I had conducted her husband's funeral under the most harrowing circumstances. She seemed much happier now

and I was glad to see this for the earlier trouble had not been of her making. It was obviously a great thrill for her to be introducing her young man.

The object of their visit was to arrange for their wedding in about six weeks' time. Having taken a note of time and place I said to them that I would be reporting the matter to the minister on his return from holiday and that one or other of us would be there to officiate. 'If it's all the same,' said the lady with her most ingratiating smile, 'we would like awfu' much if it was you. You see,' she hastened to explain, 'you were that nice at my last man's funeral.'

I know of an incident that actually occurred in Glasgow when a little group of expectant worshippers gathered in the street outside a badly run-down city charge one Sunday only to discover that the kirk doors were all securely bolted.

They were joined by the minister, who, however, had no key and no knowledge of what had happened to the beadle. Hopefully, they stood around for a little, but the day was cold, a heavy downpour seemed none too distant, and there was no indication that the doors would ever open. Unanimously it was agreed to call it a day, but before dispersing they 'uplifted the offering'. If it was not an act of worship at least it was a gesture in the direction of the Almighty.

Which, incidentally, reminds me of a day early in my career as an Assistant when I went to visit an elderly member who hadn't been too well. The door was opened by her daughter who greeted me, 'Oh, you're the man about the fire insurance, come in.' My remark as I followed her into the kitchen, 'Yes, but not quite the fire insurance you're thinking of,' was, I'm afraid quite lost and I had to explain my identity in more straightforward terms.

There is the tale of the wedding guest who thought to pass the time till the bride's arrival with a smoke and lit up accordingly. The beadle leapt upon him. Extinguishing the fag which he lodged behind his ear for a later occasion, he turned to his neighbour. 'What d'ye think's got into him?' This gentleman was better informed in ecclesiastial rules, 'It's got to do wi' their insurance,' he explained. The would-be smoker was satisfied.

It is said by the cynic that most people have a connection with some Church – even it's only the Church they stay away from. In spite of the best efforts of the ecumenists it is surely true to say of some that they get as much edification out of their dislike and distrust of the denomination they do not support as from the one to which they are nominally attached. That is what lends the peculiar punch and bite to this little story which, unless seen against that background, must seem as meaningless as it is apocryphal.

He was a twentieth-century Robinson Crusoe and he had spent thirty years marooned on an uncharted island in the Pacific. Till one day, in the best story-book tradition, a ship put in for fresh water and he was 'discovered'. Before leaving the island that had been for so long his home he was proudly showing his rescuers some of the things he had done and made.   In particular there was the remarkably fine house he had built for himself. When this had been duly admired he said, 'And now I should like you to come and see my little Church.' He led the way to a little building quite like a kirk in design, furnished in the most discreet and seemly taste.

'Every Sunday,' he explained, 'I come down here, I read a passage of Scripture, and I say a prayer, and usually I sing a verse or two of a hymn. Throughout my captivity having this Church to come to has helped me more than I can ever tell.' Much impressed the little company was filing out of the Church when the Captain was intrigued to notice a not dissimilar structure nearby. 'Excuse me, he said, 'but that building over there, that too looks rather like a Church.' 'Oh yes,' said Robinson with the air of a man who has just detected a bad smell, 'that is the Church I do not go to.'

Talking of ecumenism turns one's mind towards the area where the efforts of that movement are most urgently needed – to the bitter and acrimonious relationship that often exists, particularly in the West of Scotland, between 'Romans' and 'Proddies' – Roman Catholics and Protestants, known also as 'Dannies' and 'Billies' – which finds its most regular outlet, and often most entertaining if not uplifting expression on the terracing at the fitba'. There is certainly no want of stories in this department, some of them funny, some of them essentially kindly, some of them just sick. My principal interest at the moment is in those characterised by the quality of being very near the bone.

Of the purely entertaining type there is this nice little tale about false decoding.

A priest paying his regular visit to his ward in hospital was complaining that this week almost every bed seemed to be occupied by 'one of our people'. Sister to whom he was speaking and who herself belonged to 'these people' manifested some surprise. 'Yes,' he said, displaying the card, 'no fewer than twenty-six Catholics and only six Protestants – a most unusually high proportion.'

Sister consulted the card. 'No, no, Father,' she consoled him, 'you've got it wrong. That's the breakfast list you're holding. P stands for Porridge and RC for Rice Crispies.'

Or there's the tale of the boy on the terracing who was shouting his head off in condemnation of Rome and all her works. 'You are a Protestant, then,' enquired the stranger standing at his elbow. 'Of course I'm a Protestant.' 'Which Church do you go to?' 'Aw here, I don't go to the kirk – I'm no' a fanatic.'

That, I would suggest, is near enough to the bone to hurt as well as to amuse, and the trouble is you can't just dismiss it as an attempt at being funny. It belongs to the same family as this rather less pointed story regarding the identification of a portrait of a famous personality.

Two strangers sat together on the terracing at a football match. As the game proceeded it became clear that one of them, if not an actively dedicated supporter of the Protestant Church, was at least a bitter enemy of the Church of Rome. During the interval they got to talking quite a bit, and when they were leaving the ground after the match the anti-Rome chap explained that he lived close by and suggested they might go to his house for a refreshment to round off the afternoon. The invitation was accepted.

Arrived at the modest residence the stranger was shown into the room while his host went to the kitchen to prepare the drinks – that is to say to add the slightest sensation of water to the whisky. As he sat in the room the stranger was amazed to find looking benignly down upon him from above the fireplace an enormous portrait of the Pope in the full splendour of his office with adornments and accoutrements to match. He couldn't believe he had got the conversation wrong, for it wasn't easy to reconcile the attitude at the match with this portrait in its place of honour.

As they sat with their drinks recalling the match the stranger took the chance of raising the religious issue and of expressing his surprise at the portrait of His Holiness. 'Ye tell me that's the Pope,' spluttered the horrified host. 'It canna be. Are you absolutely sure.'

The stranger explained it was a well-known portrait held in highest esteem, and even veneration in some quarters. 'Wait till I get my hauns on Tom Shanks,' said his enraged host. 'When he sold me that picture for £20 he swore it was Rabbie Burns in his full Masonic regalia. Juist wait till I get my hauns on him – I'll regalia him.'

Or at least so the story goes.

It is no part of the bigotry based on religious fanaticism to say that the Church of Rome takes a totally different position from the churches of the Reformation in regard to gambling and the profits arising therefrom. Money is power and the important question is the use to which it is put, not the source from which it has come. As one priest is alleged to have explained when asked whether he would accept a donation from funds he knew to have been acquired in some-what doubtful fashion, 'There's nothin' the matter there that a good blessin' wouldn't cure.'

Again it is the same attitude – in reverse perhaps this time – that is illustrated in the following yarn.

Two young priests had just won a vast fortune on the pools and this had been accorded the full measure of publicity that usually attends such an event. A few nights later the pair of them were seated at a table covered with correspondence when they were joined by the old priest. They talked a little about their good fortune and its side effects. 'What's worrying us, Father,' said one of them pointing to the mass of letters on the table, 'is that we can't make up our minds what we should do about all the usual begging letters.' Oh,' said the old priest, 'don't let that worry you – just send them out as usual.'

Talking of the income from lotteries brings to mind some of the many jokes told of those who have won vast fortunes on the pools. Some people, catapulted into a situation where they possess wealth which defies their most elementary knowledge of arithmetic to comprehend, a situation for coping with whose demands they have no training whatever – such people are to be pitied, I'm sure, rather than either envied or laughed at. To add to their problem there's the massive publicity that invariably surrounds them, not to mention the company of blood-suckers of one sort or another that instantly descends upon them. Often I think that the winners in these affairs deserve our sympathy far more than do the losers. After all the latter were living up to their own expectations and well within their own capacities and needed little sympathy. The following tale is good-natured, even if it has that element of truth that brings it into the category with which I'm dealing.

It was clear that the couple were accustomed to modest ways, but through the mysterious working of the football pool system they had come into a vast fortune. Never having been out of the country they decided for starters to treat themselves to the most palatial thing in cruises the pictorial magazines could suggest.

A few days at sea and the captain was discussing with the chief steward the question of who might be invited to share his table that evening at dinner. The passenger list was a bit thin on celebrities so the steward suggested that the couple – whose good fortune had been so lavishly reported in the media – would provide company for the evening that would be out of the usual run and might well prove interesting. The captain agreed.

But a surprise was in store for the steward when he presented the Master's compliments and hoped they would find it convenient to come to the Captain's table for dinner. 'Is our money not as good as other people's?' enquired the outraged tourist. 'Why should we be expected to eat with the crew?'

The army, with its rigid attitude to discipline, its horror of initiative, its clamping down on any attempt to step out of line, its whole ethos of keeping in step and certainly not reasoning why, theirs but to do or die, tends very easily to the kind of humour of which I have been speaking. The following little tale is surely a case in point.

The scene is set in an Army Recruiting Office during the War at a time when great numbers of civilians were being called up for medical inspection. One man, having undergone the full rigours of the examination was given a line to take to another address where he would have his eyes tested. He was to return and simply hand in the report with which, he was assured, the optician would supply him.

Presenting himself some time later with the optician's report in his hand he was shown into a cubicle and told by the sergeant major that he was to strip. Patiently he explained that he had already undergone the full nudist treatment and that all he had now to do was to hand over a scrap of paper. The man in uniform indicated that he couldn't care less what he had been doing in the past, his sole concern was with what he was to be doing right now and that was simply to be getting into the cubicle and getting out of his clothes.

The unhappy man was beginning a third attempt at an explanation, but his eyesight, however defective, was good enough for him to see big trouble approaching. So obediently he entered the cubicle and fulfilled instructions. Emerging in much the condition in which his mother had first beheld him (except that on the earlier occasion he had no optician's report) he took his place at the end of a long queue of 'streakers' like himself. Still smarting from the injusice of it all he began to tell his tale to the man immediately in front of him in the line. 'I don't know what you think you've got to girn about,' said that nudist-by-instruction, 'I'm here from the Post Office trying to deliver a telegram.'

Those who have been victims of the 'permission to speak, Sir' system will respond very sharply to the story of the Spit and Polish Oracle.

It was an army computer of the very latest design with which the General had been supplied. He decided to seek its help in a difficult decision with which he was confronted, so he fed in all the information about his own forces, their dispositions, the strength of their armament, the nature of the terrain, and then also, so far as was known to him, the corresponding information in regard to the enemy. Then he posed the all-important question, 'Shall I advance, or had I better retreat?' The usual whirring of wheels and blinking of lights and then on to the screen there flashed the simple message – 'Yes'. This the General found rather less than helpful. So he fed in the supplementary question, 'Yes, what?' Instantly there flashed on the answer, 'Yes, sir.'

At least he was in no worse plight than the officer in charge of a small party who sent back word by telegram, 'Am going to advance; stop; send reinforcements.' For when this reached its destination it read, 'Am going to a dance; Stop; send three and fourpence.'

It's many a long year since Punch produced the unforgettable cartoon that showed two farmers, one at either end of a cow, the man at the head pulling manfully at the halter, the other straining no less manfully by means of a kinch in the tail. Meanwhile a lawyer sat comfortably and contentedly on a stool getting on with the milking.

A popular theme, this, of the lawyer's keeping the litigation going for his own rather than his client's sake. I'm sure it's a completely defamatory tale about a most honourable profession with no grain of truth in it – this story of 'The Fleecing'.

A dispute had arisen between two prosperous sheep-farmers about a transacton just completed in the cattle-market at Perth. They were on the point of settling their argument by resort to fisticuffs when one of them was half dragged away from the scene by his friend. Not unnaturally the friend took him to a nearby hostelry to see whether the fires of hostility that were raging so furiously could be quenched by the liquid available there. He was not wholly successful, but at length he got his man to agree that the law was the thing to which to turn in such a case. Unhappily the victim did not have a lawyer. Not to worry, said his mate, he had a lawyer, and a damned good lawyer at that, and they would just go and see him now and have the matter put in hand without more delay. They could then enjoy their dram with some peace of mind.

So off they set for the office of the lawyer to whom they told their story. 'I'm very sorry,' said he, 'I should have been more than delighted to act for your friend, but as it happens the other party to the dispute is a client of mine and it's not half-an-hour since he was here seeking advice and instructing me to act for him.'

The friends were distinctly discomfitted.

'If you are worried about finding another solicitor I can very easily give you a note of introduction to a colleague who, I'm sure, would be more than happy to take up your case and for whose professional skill I have the highest regard. Oh yes, your case would be secure in his hands.'

The suggestion was taken up with alacrity. The lawyer wrote a little note, put it in an envelope which he carefully sealed, and on which he wrote the name and address of his friend. Now it is a well-established fact that trailing round lawyers' offices is a drouthie affair, so the worthies decided that before visiting this other firm another 'strengthener' was called for. This led to another and then to another. By now they were gaining in assurance as well as increasing in stature. They decided they had better see what was in the letter. It gave a brief account of the circumstances leading to the threatened litigation, explained that the writer was committed to one side, and hoped that the recipient would espouse the cause of the other. And it ended with the couplet

> *Two woolly ewes frae the Braes o' Balquhidder*
> *You fleece the ane an' I'll fleece the ither.*

While the point can be much exaggerated in the popular mind there can still be no doubt that the winding up of estates is a reasonably profitable branch of the practice of law. Which explains the tale of the solicitor sitting in his accustomed corner of the compartment in the morning train engrossed in the day's paper, with particular concern for the obituary column, who threw down his paper on the seat with the disgusted comment 'Not a death worth a damn.'

It's when nice legal points emerge in course of the winding up that it becomes really worth while from the point of view both of interest and of income. It has to be conceded, of course, that the complications do not originate in the winding-up but are inherent in the testamentary instrument itself. That is why it used to be said that the first toast after 'The Queen' at every self-respecting Faculty Dinner was 'The Man who Makes His Own Will'. And the second was like unto it, 'To the Firm which Produces the Printed Will Forms.' Between them they have been responsible for a lot of profitable business. Things, however, must have got to a fairly advanced stage when this incident occurred.

Two lawyers were discussing a will – one of the kind where a lot of money was at stake and that raised a number of complicated legal issues – the kind of will that leads to the proverbial saying that 'Where there's a will there's a way – to the lawyers'.

At some length they discussed this point and that, in some detail they argued how the court might react to this principle and how far to that precedent. The discussion was brought to a fitting close with the sentiment, 'At least it seems highly unlikely that any of the fortune will get frittered away among the beneficiaries.'

You can't blame it all on the lawyers, for there are those who blithely sell themselves into slavery on the litigation treadmill, the Dandie Dinmonts of this world who are never happy unless they have a guid gangin' plea in one court or another. Such folk are a boon to the legal profession, they can be humoured with so little encouragement. Take, for instance, the nameless hero of the tale, 'Where Do I Go Now?'

It was an exceedingly angry man who called at the solicitor's office demanding to see a lawyer. When at length he got an audience he explained the reason for his wrath. Having entered into a contract with one he thought to be his friend he had been very ill treated. He counted on the courts to secure justice for him.

The lawyer, though deeply sympathetic towards the man for the way in which he had been treated, was not able whole-heartedly to share the view that in law he had suffered an injustice. He indicated that while it was possible for an action to be raised, the outcome of a case in court was far from a foregone conclusion, and considerable expense might well be incurred. Expense, the client indcated, represented no difficulty. The scoundrel who had done this despicable thing must be taken to the cleaners.

The lawyer agreed to raise an action in the Sheriff Court and the client blithely put him in funds to a modest extent. Having lost his case here the man came storming back angrier than ever. 'Where do I go now?' was his sole concern. One possible answer was that he should go home and forget the whole affair, the other was to go on appeal to the Court of Session. Without hesitation the client plumped for the latter course, putting the lawyer in funds, this time to the tune of £800.

Once again in the fullness of time judgment was given against him with expenses and once again he arrived furious in the lawyer's office demanding to know, 'Where do I go now?' It was pointed out that appeal could be taken to the Inner House but that the costs would be unpredictable. This proved no deterrent and once again funds were made available.

The Division having upheld the judgment of the Outer House the obvious question was, 'Where do I go now?' and the equally clear answer was 'To the House of Lords.' This time some £3000 was made available to meet preliminary outgoings. The supreme court of the land having seen no reason to depart from the conclusion reached with what was becoming monotonous regularity elsewhere, the still far-from-satisfied client appeared at the office with his standard enquiry, 'Where do I go now?'

'My good friend,' replied the solicitor, 'where you must go now is into society and find yourself a charming young wife, and waste no time in having a real big family. Believe me, the law needs men of your stamp.'

In this connection I may be forgiven for interjecting that I have occasionally commented to friends in the legal world on what has always appealed to me as an unjust practice of the law. Let us suppose that in the foregoing tale the House of Lords had seen fit to recall the judgment reached in all the lower courts and to find in favour of the appellant, then his unhappy opponent who had been consistently winning all along the line would find himself saddled with the entire costs of the whole litigation – and that with no other court in which to seek redress. It seems perfectly reasonable that if a man insists on raising – or defending – an insupportable case he should take the consequences of his fool-hardiness and meet the costs needlessly incurred. The loser pays.

But if his case has stood up before the Sheriff and the two divisions it can scarcely be called 'insupportable'.

The final judgment may even, for example, declare that the Sheriff 'misdirected himself in law' on a certain point, or that 'their Lordships in the Inner House put too much trust on the evidence of the witness Smith.' So the continuance of the litigation was not at all due to the intransigence of the litigant; it was wholly due to the incompetence of the bench. Hard, is it not, that the bill should appear on the defender's plate.

My friends in the profession, I may say, invariably see this kind of comment as one coming very near to the bone but as being not the least bit funny. Were I the unsuccessful litigant I should not find it the least bit funny either!

It is not by any means just ministers or lawyers who are the victims of this kind of sharp-edged humour. The psychiatrist of today comes in – understandably in my view – for a good deal of humour that is cutting rather than just funny. The crack, for example, that the difference between the psychiatrist and his patient is that there is a hope, however slender, that the latter may recover.

Modern art too has its detractors functioning in the field of fun. Maybe, of course, that is a good thing, for there are some subjects that are best not taken too seriously. I confess to a certain affection for the story of the Baffled Baddies – probably because I can so well understand their plight.

Three hoodlums had joined the Youth Club attached to the local kirk. They had a considerable reputation for mischief and were thought to specialise in vandalism. The minister had given them a lecture about trying to do something constructive which, he claimed, could prove every bit as interesting and exciting as smashing and destroying. They should begin by trying to broaden and improve their minds. 'For example,' he concluded, 'there's a collection of modern art on show in the Town Hall this week. Why not go in there one day and just study the pictures. You'll enjoy it I promise you.' His audience seemed a trifle sceptical.

A few days later, however, it was pouring with rain and they were at a loose end and so, there being nothing handy for them to break, the leader suggested a visit to see thae picturs the minister had been talking about. So to the Town Hall they bent their steps.

The first picture looked as though someone had taken the works of a grandfather clock apart and scattered the pieces around on a chequered cloth which covered a table whose legs sprawled in different directions. It bore the title 'Reclining Nude'. Having devoted a little study to this masterpiece they moved to Exhibit No 2. This consisted of a series of geometrical figures – circles, squares, triangles, rhombuses, the lot – in a variety of bright colours and bore the title 'West Highland Sunset'.

The third picture was quite startling. One formed the impression that someone had covered a canvas with a fairly thick coat of an unpleasant shade, smearing a quantity of red in the centre. Without waiting to see what this was called the leader of the group said to his pals, 'Come on, boys, let's get away oot o' here. We'll be gettin' blamed for this.'

My other tale in this field has nothing to do with modern art as such but is, it seems to me, an interesting reflection on the attitude of so many to art in any of its forms. Some would call it a pathetic tale, and so I imagine it is. But that would seen to underline just how near it comes to being an expression of reality.

It was near to the town of Kirkcudbright that a friend of mine who belongs to the colony of artists inhabiting that quarter had stopped to admire the view. Inspired by what he saw he drew out a sketching-pad and squatted down by the side of the road to get it all down. He was vaguely conscious of the fact that this activity was the subject of some interest to a man who was ploughing with a pair of horses in the field at his back. Always when they got to the headrig the horses were stopped for a minute or two and my friend had the impression of being critically surveyed by the ploughman from over the hedge.

Ultimately on the occasion of one of these stops the horses were left to their own devices and the ploughman appeared at the elbow of the sketcher, a clay pipe in the corner of his cheek, an open pen-knife protruding between the thumb and forefinger of his right hand while a fill of thick black tobacco was being assiduously rubbed in the palm of his left hand.

'You're makin' a pictur,' was the countryman's opening gambit. My friend explained that was not quite his object – he was making a sketch from which at some later time something might possibly emerge.

'It's a wonder ye never thocht to get yersel a camera,' persisted his critic. My friend admitted that he did possess a camera, but that had little relevance to his present pursuit. He went on to give a lecture in what he considered the simplest terms about the difference between the mechicanical reproduction which the lens of a camera can supply and the delicate work of interpretation which supervenes when the lens happens to be that of a human eye.

By this time the man of the fields had got his pipe filled and a match applied. 'Ah weel,' said he between puffs, 'mebbe that, ay, mebbe that. But I'm thinkin, the camera wad be a lot quicker . . .' and after a few puffs '. . . an' a damn sight liker the thing when ye were feenished.'

By way of bringing this chapter to a close I should like to add a little miscellany of jokes all of which satisfy the characteristic of gaining their whole point from being so true a reflection of, as well as an extremely sharp commentary upon, some aspect of life. There's this tale from the West Highlands, for instance, indicating with clarity just how far and how deep sex discrimination has penetrated these northern fastnesses.

It was clear for all to behold that the crofter was in acute pain as he hirpled into the doctor's surgery at Invermuckle. 'Well, my friend,' he was greeted, 'and what have you been up to that's got you into this sad state?'

'Ach, doctor, it's my back. I haff the most terrible pain wheneffer I get up in the morning, and it doesn't get a bit better as the day goes on. I'm not even comfortable when I'm in my bed.'

'You'd better take your things off and let me have a look at you.' After due inspection the doctor explained that the back had been strained, adding, 'But Hamish, you must have been conscious of this at the time you did it.'

'Ach yes, doctor, fine I ken how I came to get it. It was the day before yesterday and we were out at the peats. There was this great creel of peats – it was far too heavy – and I was lifting it to put in on my wife's shoulder for her to carry home when I felt the pain

53

gripping me. I shouldn't have been doing it – I knew at the time it was far too heavy.'

The following is a rather touching tale, is it not, of the young student reconciling himself to the thought of having to resit his examinations in September.

It was one of these examinations that allowed for a good deal of discursive writing on each of the seven topics which it offered for consideration. To keep the enthusiasm of the candidate within limits it was stated that not more than four questions should be attempted.

One of the papers when it got into the hands of the examiners showed a first question answered in great detail, the English of impeccable literary excellence, the handwriting near to copperplate. The second question was answered equally fully, but the language was slipshod, all sorts of contractions were used, and the handwriting steadily deteriorated throughout. When it came to the third question 'to be attempted' it was seen that the answer consisted of a single sheet with the bones of a fairly adequate treatment set forth under a series of sketchy headings.

On turning over yet again the examiner found himself confronted with a neat square drawn in the centre of the page and printed therein in block letters:

WATCH THIS SPACE IN SEPTEMBER.

It might indeed be argued that the real characteristic of the kind of joke with which I'm dealing here is that it has a moral to teach, that it is kind of parable. That is surely supremely true in the following instance. I've used it myself as a sermon illustration – which I shouldn't be prepared to do with them all!

A little boy was pushing a four-wheeled barrow up one of the steep streets with which the town of Greenock is so richly endowed. After a while he set down the barrow, sat on its trams, and proceeded to 'draw his breath'.

A gentleman who had been watching the youngster's efforts came forward at this point and said to him, 'Look, sonny, you should never push a barrow up a hill. In that way you are wasting a great deal of effort through simply pushing the barrow into the hill. What you ought always to do is to pull the barrow, for in that way the line of traction runs parallel with the line of travel and so the entire output of energy is directed towards producing results.'

Clearly the gentleman was a cross between a student of dynamics and an expert in time-and-motion study.

The little chap, however, seemed remarkably unimpressed. Getting off his seat and into pushing position exactly as before he spat on his hands, lifted the trams of the barrow, and said, 'Ach, Mister, wad ye no' gi'es a wee shove.'

Here's another one with a sting in its tail. For all that it sounds a bit unlikely it comes remarkably near the mark, a reminder that, try as you will, you cannot recreate the past.

The couple had enjoyed fifty years of married bliss and were agreed that such an achievement demanded suitable recognition. The lady, to whom not unnaturally the matter of making arrangements had been remitted with powers, was of a romantic disposition and decided to mark the occasion in a quite unique way. So she organised a short Service of Thanksgiving to be conducted in the Church where the wedding had taken place. This was followed by a modest reception for friends and descendants of the original guests in the very room where the wedding dinner had been served. Even the menu was a reproduction from fifty years before – the price being the only thing that was different. And then as a crowning glory to the whole performance she had reserved the bridal suite in the hotel where they had spent the first night of their honeymoon.

All this unusual excitement at his age had had its inevitable effect on the male partner so that when at length they got to their bedroom he asked for nothing more than to be allowed to lay his head gently on the pillow and say 'Goodnight'.

Jean, however, had other ideas. 'Willie,' she reproved him, 'ye're surely no' goin' to sleep without gi'en me a bit cuddle. Dae ye no' mind that first nicht you were keen enough to gi'e me a cuddle.' Rousing himself Willie did his best to mount a display of ardour and enthusiasm, if not perhaps of consuming passion. His duty done he was about to seek forgetfulness in slumber. 'Dae ye mind what ye did that nicht efter ye gi'ed me a cuddle?' persisted his tormentor. As Willie seemed unable – or perhaps unwilling – she prompted him, 'Ach ye're bound to mind that – ye bit my ear.'

At that William leapt out of bed. 'What's the matter?' enquired an alarmed Jean. 'Whaur are ye awa' tae?' 'I'm awa' through tae the bathroom to get my teeth.'

As I have said so often already you cannot recreate the past. The passion you may be able, with an effort, to simulate; but the teeth once gone are on a plate for ever. It's a lesson that all of us, as we grow relentlessly older, could profitably take to heart. And, if I may dare to say so, it is a lesson that conservationists could usefully keep at the back of their minds. Let's try to create a future, not to recreate a past.

The following account of an incident at a Burns Supper in the bard's own country is one of my favourites.

The Burns Supper in the village hall was progressing according to the best tradition for such events. Full justice had been done to the haggis and the numerous and varied toasts had not been neglected. The company of country folk had got to that stage where they were ready to appreciate to the full a rendering of Burns' 'Ode to a Mouse'.

As the elocutionist pulled out all the stops in portraying the unhappy lot of the 'wee sleekit cooerin' tim'rous beastie' left homeless to face November's sleaty drizzle and cranreuch cauld there wasn't a dry eye in the hall. How right the Bard had been to regret that disturbance of nature's social union that makes the poor creature startle 'at me their poor earth-born companion and fellow-mortal'.

Unbeknown to the company, however, there was, sheltering behind the wainscoating just such a timorous beastie which, emboldened presumably by this welter of sympathy, bonhomie, and general good fellowship so freely extended towards it and its kind, ventured out into the hall where it darted from the shelter of one female skirt to that of another. Instantly chairs were pushed back and the whole company was in an uproar, the women leaping on to chairs in terror, the men folk stamping about in tackety boots shouting, 'Get the dirty wee vermin!' – or some such phrase.

There is a lot of sting there, isn't there. Tears for the mouse of the poem; tackety boots for the mouse of reality. There are so many things in life which appear one way when they afflict our neighbour but in a quite different way when they come close to our own doors. Apartheid in South Africa is one thing, a black family moving in next door is quite another thing.

I conclude this chapter with what must surely be one of the nastiest cracks I have ever heard, and effective just because it comes so horribly near to the truth.

> The motor industry had been enjoying one of its not infrequent stoppages – it was the victim of what is not very accurately called 'industrial action'. A man was passing the factory gate when he spied a friend sitting on an upturned oil drum, warming his hands at a brazier while studying the racing pages of the paper.
>
> 'Hallo, Bobbie,' he greeted him, 'what dae ye think ye're daein' there?'
>
> 'I'm here on picket duty,' was the reply.
>
> 'O I see. So the strike's still on. When I saw you sittin' there daein' nothin' I thocht you must be back at your work.'

CHAPTER FIVE

COULD HAVE BEEN BETTER PUT

A GENEROUS CONTRIBUTION TO the merriment of mankind has been supplied – unintentionally and unconsciously – by those with a limited command of the language. I do not refer merely to Mrs Malaprop and her kind, though they have done their bit. It is amazing how people have contrived by the use of the misrelated phrase and by the unhappy juxtaposition of unrelated ideas to produce some ridiculous and highly entertaining pictures. This particular brand of humour can come very near to the schoolboy howler, but while they are very closely related they are not identical.

The classical example, I'm sure, is the newspaper advertisement for the sale of a dog among whose admirable qualities was listed, 'will eat anything, very fond of children'.

It is from more modern times and a source from which better things might have been expected that there comes the perfect gem – which I believe to be true.

The notice appeared in the window of the local authority of a small country town. It was headed PEST CONTROL and it read:

> 'The Council regret that it has been found necessary to impose a small charge for the services of the Pest Control Officer in the extermination of lice, bugs, beetles, mice, rats and other vermin. Old Age Pensioners free of charge.'

The same kind of unhappy juxtaposition turns what should have been a quite solemn account for services rendered into a highly entertaining picture of a self-defeating exercise. The local country joiner had been called in to deal with an offensive smell in the sitting-room of one of the village houses. This he did smartly and efficiently, later sending an account which read – 'To lifting floorboards in sitting room, removing dead rat and replacing same £2.50'.

An album could be filled with copies of 'notes' sent to school-teachers to excuse the absence of pupils on account, frequently, of the illness of the mother who may have been described as doing anything from 'hanging on to the mantelpiece with her kidneys' to being 'in bed with the doctor' or even in one case to 'crawling all over the kitchen floor with the plumber'. But I think it would be hard to excel a 'note' the original manuscript of which a retired school-teacher pal of mine treasures very dearly. It is in these terms:

'Dear Teacher – Please excuse Willie not being at school yesterday for he had to stay at home and help with the children being as how his mother had just had a new baby and oblidge.
P S – It was not the boy's fault.'

It is not just to teachers that small boys have sometimes to convey notes. I am reminded of the delightful yarn that might be given the title, 'One Bad Egg Begets Another'.

A small boy presented himself at the local store, conveying to the shopkeeper a note which read, 'Out of the dozen eggs I bought in your shop this morning two are completely rotten. If you are not prepared to take my word I can send the eggs along to prove it.'

In due course the boy returned home with two fresh eggs and also a fresh note which read, 'Regret to hear about the bad eggs which I am replacing. Don't trouble to send the bad ones along – your word is every bit as good as the eggs.'

Very often it is the unhappy choice of a word that leads to the smile, though in this case it is on the double significance of a word that the joke turns.

The workman was retiring from the firm after forty years of devoted service. A farewell had been arranged for the presentation of gifts – flowers for the man's wife, a cheque to allow for a holiday, and a time-piece (to be carefully distinguished from a mere clock) which, ticking away on the mantelshelf, would act as a constant reminder of these forty faithful years.

The gifts were being handed over by the foreman who felt

constrained to use the occasion to comment upon the transience earthly things – the flowers were so very lovely for a day or two, the cheque might last for a little while but sooner rather than later it would go too. 'But,' he concluded, triumphantly placing his hand upon the timepiece, 'this I promise you, this will never go.'

The following tale follows the same pattern, but in this case it is the unhappy choice of a figure of speech rather than of a wrong word that opens up the possibility so quickly exploited by the man with a nimble brain.

A priest and a minister were chatting together in a corner of the room. Waiters were circulating with trays of drinks. One of these approached them, 'Will you have a glass of whisky, Father?' The priest helped himself. 'And a whisky for you, Minister?' The minister was scandalised. 'I would not touch that stuff,' he protested. 'Take it away.' He went on to elaborate his point by adding, 'I would as soon be seen committing adultery as drinking whisky.' Hurriedly the priest returned his glass to the tray – 'I didn't know there was a choice,' he explained.

This tale conforms to the same general pattern the difference being that here the humour lies in the implication that otherwise the occasion would have been such a happy and satisfying one.

She knew she was dying, poor soul, and she was making some final arrangements with her husband regarding the details of her forthcoming funeral. 'In the first coach,' she said,'there'll be you and the children and my mother . . .'

'Afore ye go ony further,' interrupted the prospective widower, 'me and yer mother are no' travellin' in the same coach. If she has to go in the first coach I'm quite prepared to travel in the second. But no' in the same yin.'

'Ach, Willie,' she said, 'I ken you an' my mither have never hit it off. But ye'll no' have her to put up wi' much longer. Surely you could manage to sit alongside her as far as the cemetery for juist this once.'

'No,' replied William with mulish obstinacy, 'ye can forget it. If she's to be there, count me out.'

'Willie,' she pleaded, 'I'll never be askin' you to do anything for me ever again. Surely you're no' going to deny me my last dying wish.'

'Well, of course, if ye put it like that,' said her husband, softening visibly, 'I canna very weel say No. But I'll tell ye this, it'll be a spoiled funeral for me.'

If what you want is an example of how an admirably organised and executed funeral can be brought to an ignominious end in sorrow and sadness it's to Ireland you go and read of the tragedy that marred a happy occasion in a village there.

The grand Irish gentleman had died, full of years and covered in honours. The local community in mourning his passing, had paid full regard to all the local traditions. There had been a wake and liquor had been consumed in prodigious quantities. So that when the time came for the actual interment it was seen as the climax of a long period of preparation. Everybody was present. After the lowering of the coffin the vast company began slowly to file past the foot of the grave. It was then that disaster struck. A young man, overcome by his grief, or, as some might have thought, a trifle unsteady after the wake, lost his balance, fell into the grave, and broke his neck. Having given a detailed account of the occurrence the local paper went on to say, 'This unfortunate accident cast a gloom over the whole proceedings.'

A good funeral spoilt, one could not but agree.

A Session Clerk is an individual who may be expected to place a high value on accuracy – after all his job is to keep the record straight – but there can arise unfortunate circumstances where one may be forgiven the background detail, however factually accurate, and satisfy oneself with a more general picture.

The elder had been in hospital for close on a fortnight when he received a visit from the Session Clerk who explained that he brought with him the greetings and good wishes of the Kirk Session as a whole.

'That was exceedingly kind and thoughtful of them,' said the appreciative invalid.

'Yes,' enlarged the Session Clerk, 'it was reported at the meeting on Tuesday that you were in hospital and by a majority of five votes to four it was resolved that I was to visit you and convey their good wishes for a speedy recovery.'

Among my own earliest experiences as a preacher there was an encounter with a Session Clerk accompanied by a fellow elder that I will not readily forget. As a story it might well be called 'Statutory Vote of Thanks'.

I was a student at the time and glad of any opportunity of gaining pulpit experience. When I was called upon at very short notice to take a service for a minister who had suddenly taken ill I was happy to do so. I preached what I considered a 'blinder' of a sermon. At that stage in one's career one is liable to think in that way. I was not at all taken by surprise therefore when after service the Session Clerk with another elder came round to the vestry to thank me. Said the Clerk, 'I just wanted to say how much we had all enjoyed the service,' and he warmly shook my hand. His understudy followed suit, remarking 'And I wanted to say I thought it was a splendid sermon.'

'You know, gentlemen, this is extraordinarily generous of you,' I acknowledged. 'Well it's like this,' explained the Session Clerk, 'our minister says that in a lot of kirks a preacher gets coming and going and nobody so much as says he's there. It's a rule with us that the two elders on duty at the door come to the vestry afterwards and say how much they enjoyed the service.'

Exactly what the lady had in mind in the undernoted exchange is clear enough in all conscience – it's just that she might have found a more kindly way of expressing it. She was visiting her friend who was very ill indeed and whom she hadn't been to see for a week or two. She was anxious not to be thought remiss in this regard.

'Although I haven't managed to get to see you, you mustn't imagine I haven't been thinking about you. I never lift the paper in the morning but I look the Deaths.'

We had in Glasgow Presbytery a minister whom I'll call M'Adam who suffered from a desire to give you the whole truth – not just the pleasant bits. I came to refer to his best efforts as 'M'Adamisms'. He'd come up to you after you had made a speech at the Assembly perhaps – 'That was a first-class speech,' he would affirm, 'really a fine effort.' And then he would go on, 'I wonder you didn't think to add . . .' or perhaps, 'I thought it was maybe a pity you put in that bit about . . .' Or just when you were feeling proud about being given some appointment along would come M'Adam with a great show of affection to say how pleased he was, and so on. Then he would add, 'The only reason I turned it down myself was . . .'

It's perhaps not quite so bad as the person who says, 'My, I was fairly sticking up for you today. There were two fellows in this pub, and they were giving you your character. One of them said you hadn't the brains of a flea. I didn't let him away with that – I said that you had.'

For some reason which I cannot explain, ministers are particularly liable to be the subject of back-handed compliments. A simple malapropism can add to the effect. The minister, he explained, says he's going to be retiring soon and some of us elders thought we'd like to get him up a wee bit momentum.'

Or again the effect may be produced by an unhappy linking of ideas – as in this case. A well-known firm of removal contractors had been invited to submit an estimate for the minister's flitting. They did so. They thanked the Session for their 'esteemed enquiry'; they indicated their price: they promised to give the matter their very best attention: and then they added a postscript, 'We may claim that in the past thirty years we have removed no fewer than twenty-six ministers to the complete satisfaction of all concerned.'

The words 'ignorant' and 'learned' would normally be accepted as antonyms – and yet there can be shades of meaning attaching to each which lead to a situation where their use as opposites will produce the most alarming effects.

He hadn't been in his first charge – a rural one – all that long, when an anniversary came round demanding special services and he arranged for one of his professors to preach by way of marking the occasion. He was still young enough to believe this would be a real treat for his people. In course of the following week he was talking to an old chap in the parish, a most faithful attender and something of a sermon-taster. 'And how did you enjoy the professor on Sunday?' he enquired. 'O he was verra guid, awfu' learned, ay, awfu' learned. But dae ye ken what I'm gonna tell ye – ye're every bit as guid yersel' – and then he added, 'in yer ain ignorant kind o' way.'

It is precisely the same kind of unfortunate choice of terms that lends point to this joke from the mental hospital – source of many a story. I take it that everybody knows about the breezy speaker who began his oration to the inmates, 'Well now, I wonder why we're all here?' only to get the instant response, 'Because we're not all there.' In this other tale, however, while it may be the patient who strikes the first blow it is the medical superintendent who delivers the *coup-de-grace*.

The chaplain was conducting a service in the mental hospital chapel on a warm Sunday afternoon. They had reached the sermon and the congregation were sitting in varying attitudes of inattention when one of them suddenly interrupted the speaker to proclaim in loud, clear tones, 'I have never heard such dreary drivel in all my life.' Before he could disgrace himself – or the hospital – any further the critic was leapt upon by three male nurses and led unprotesting from the scene, not to appear again that afternoon. The minister was able to deliver the remainder of his talk to a non-belligerent if not very attentive and none too interested audience.

Afterwards the medical superintendent was giving a most abject apology for the incident. Not to worry, said the chaplain, such things were bound to occur in a place like this. After all, the other patients didn't seem to be the least disturbed. And he himself, of course, had no hard feelings.

'But,' persisted the doctor, 'what annoys me about the whole affair is that it's the first really intelligent assessment that patient has made in years.'

This tale from the vestry might well be classified as a 'dirty crack' but I prefer to think of it as an observation made in all good faith – though it wouldn't have been any more shattering had it been made in bad faith!

'Dae ye ken,' said the beadle as he helped the young minister out of his robes in the vestry, 'ye fair remind me o' the great Dr Richmond that used to be here.' This was praise indeed, for wherever the young man turned he was deaved with tales of the pulpit prowess of this distinguished predecessor.

'And in what way,' the elated young man was foolish enough to ask, 'do I remind you of the great doctor?' (He had still to learn the lesson always to leave well alone.)

Draping the cassock over a chair the beadle explained, 'Ye sweat somethin' terrible under the oxters.'

There certainly was no want of good faith in any of the following incidents – indeed some of the good faith might have been sacrificed in favour of a little tact. I think it's the utter honesty of the comment – without fear or favour – that makes it so entertaining.

The minister was still fairly new to the parish. Visiting, not for the first time, one of his house-bound parishioners he was rising to go when she said, 'I've never gotten doon to the kirk to hear you. But noo the better days are comin' I maun try an' manage to the kirk. It's no' but what I want to come, but I'm fair crippled wi' this arthritis and in this cauld weather I never get ower the door. Noo it's a bit milder, though, I maun make the effort to get doon. For I've ay wanted to hear you.'

'I don't know,' said the preacher modestly, 'that in not hearing me you've missed very much, you know.'

'No,' she happily conceded, 'that's what everybody tells me.'

Or what about this one?

It was in a day when people were still inordinately proud of what today we contemptuously refer to as 'steam radio' and when the height of every minister's ambition was to be invited to put over a service on the air. A minister was visiting an old fellow in his congregation when in course of conversation the remark was passed, 'They havena got you on the wireless yet.' The minister, a modest man, bought it. 'No, Tom, they havena got down to my level yet.'

'Oh no,' replied Tom, 'I wadna let ye say that, they had an awfu' puir man on last Sunday.'

Nor does an encounter like the following do anything to boost the ego.

The proud mother was lamenting how terribly hard her brilliant son was having to work for his law degree examinations at the University. The idea, she declared, seemed to be to fail everybody if they could. Her hearer, anxious to be sympathetic, agreed that there was an ever-rising standard. The outlet for graduates was shrinking, so they were arranging that the supply would diminish. Hence the increasing number of those left by the wayside.

'I know,' he said, 'that even in Divinity the standard has gone up out of all recognition since I myself came through the University.' 'Maybe then,' said the lady kindly, 'it's just as well you got through when you did.'

Or again there is this wonderful story which the late Dr William Baxter used to tell at his own expense – and he was economical in his use of such material. In his case it's an element of dramatic irony that provides the driving-power for the amusement.

One Sunday evening Dr Baxter was to be conducting the evening service at the nearby Church of Wellington. This is approached from University Avenue by an enormous flight of steps leading to a great pillared portico and as the good doctor arrived he found an elderly lady beginning the laborious ascent, obviously under stress. Gallantly he went forward and, taking her by the arm he oxtered her up the stairs. Arrived at the top both paused for breath.

'Thank you very much for that help up these stairs,' said the lady, and went on to ask whether he happened to know who was to be preaching here tonight. 'Yes indeed I do,' he said, 'it's an old fellow from Dowanhill called Baxter.'

'Oh him!' she replied. Turning about she enquired, 'I wonder whether I could bother you to give me a hand back down the steps.'

An unusual way of putting a death-wish on someone is represented in this anecdote.

Mrs Fulsome was unstinted in her admiration of her minister's preaching. Why, she demanded to know, were not his sermons in print for all to read. It was a shame that such first-class material should be heard on a single Sunday only to vanish into oblivion. They were worthy not only of wider circulation but also of deeper study – he really must consider the possibility of publication. 'No, no,' the minister protested, it was nice of her to say these things, but he would never dream of going into print.

'Oh but I know they will be printed,' she insisted,' they simply must be published.'

'Well,' he conceded, 'posthumously, perhaps.'

'But that would be simply splendid,' said Mrs Fulsome – 'at least provided it's not to be too long delayed.'

To return to the simple pun there's the story of the American benefactor who felt he had a grievance. Interestingly enough it is only because two brands of the one language are involved that there is a pun. Thus the perpetrator of the gaffe could well be unaware of how clumsy he had been. But to our tale.

The American visitor had arrived in the little Highland village from which his forbears had come during the clearances to shape a new life across the ocean. He was horrified to find the kirk in a pitiful state of neglect and the graveyard so overgrown he just couldn't discover the stone marking the burial-place of his forefathers. He sought out the minister and expressed his concern.

Sorrowfully the minister conceded that things were not as he for his part would have wanted them. But then they had only a very few families left in the parish, all of them old and impoverished, so what could they do? A few years earlier they had engaged an architect and had a plan prepared for the rehabilitation of the church, but the cost had been utterly prohibitive, so the whole thing had to be shelved. Nobody regretted it more than he.

So much interest did the visitor manifest that the minister scrounged around and came up with the drawings. 'Look,' said the visitor after he had examined these, 'I'm real proud of this place. This is where my roots lie. I owe this place something. I should like to see this work done and the whole outfit put in order so that we could all take pride in it. I'm prepared to meet all the bills, for I want to see the work done.'

This was truly tremendous news. The work was put in hand and proceeded apace – at least by West Highland standards. In due course the stage was reached where a date could be fixed for the Service of Rededication. Needless to say the American benefactor was invited to attend on this occasion, and, no less needless to say, he gladly accepted the invitation. Wherever he went he was feted and fussed over and had a wonderful time. It was only when they got to the highlight of the service that disaster struck.

It was in the prayer of thanksgiving following upon the Act of Dedication that it happened. In course of this prayer the celebrant took occasion to remind the Almighty of the earlier condition of the kirk and its grounds – and now this miraculous transformation – and all due to 'this kindly succour from across the ocean.'

What a pity they hadn't had a printed Order of Service – even to an American it would have seemed all right in type, or so one imagines.

If you have a taste for the simple, straightforward pun that is in no need of a transatlantic twist, what of this delightful example of down-to-earth honesty.

The minister was accosted on the street by a man whose face was vaguely familiar – very vaguely. 'Aw but, minister, ye canna have forgotten me,' remonstrated the stranger – 'it was you that married Maggie an' me, juist ten years ago last week.' The minister offered apology. After all, he conducted many weddings and ten years was a long time. He could hardly be expected to remember every bridegroom.

'Ach,' persisted his tormentor, 'but ye couldna possibly forget oor weddin'. I was the chap that arrived at the kirk withoot the papers an' you had to keep the guests entertained for close on twa hoors till the taxi took me awa' hame for them.'

'But of course,' said the minister, 'I've got you perfctly now. My, but you got a queer fright that night.'

'Ye can say that again,' said the proud husband, 'an' what's mair, I've got her still.'

The confusion that leads to a story being funny does not always arise from the use of a particular word of double significance. The meaning of the term may be unequivocal enough, the confusion arising from the choice of object to which it refers.

The congregational fabric committee was discussing various repairs requiring to be carried out at the Church. One particular item demanded the services of a joiner and it was agreed that one should be engaged. 'Well,' said one member, 'if we've got a joiner coming I think we should take the chance and get him to make a new seat for the toilet in the kirk vestibule. The one we've got has been cracked for years, and it leaves a very bad impression – especially on visitors.'

Here is an example of something slightly different. In this case the fun arises from the fact that the hearer is lured down a completely false path, discovering his mistake much too late.

The old lady was explaining to the minister why she no longer attended the Guild meeting. 'Och ay it used to be I wouldna hae missed a meetin' for anyting. We all took oor knittin' of course but it wasna for the knittin' we went but purely for the gossip. It was terrible,' she went on, 'the way we talked aboot folk – juist pure gossip. I've stopped goin',' she added virtuously. 'Oh, it must be more than a year ago now, an' I've never been back; an' what's more I'm not going back. No, nothing but gossip. What I do now is that I just sit at my ain fireside an' get on with my knitting on my lone-some. There's no use my saying I'll come back to the Guild now. You see, I'm gettin' so deaf I canna hear a word o' what they're sayin'.'

Talking of being led up the wrong path reminds me of what I have always thought of as an outstanding example of a funny story – not the kind that will produce a great rumbling guffaw but the sort rather that gently tickles the palate. The child's description of the disaster is so telling!

The American was proud and happy to be visiting the land of his birth. He had been a babe in arms when his parents had emigrated to the New World and this was his first chance to visit the old one. With the aid of a Glasgow solicitor he had managed to unearth a good deal of family background – enough eventually to justify a visit to this little Dumfriesshire village in one of whose modest dwellings he had first seen the light of day.

A little bit of enquiring here and there among some of the older residents, not to mention a few drams in the Black Bull to help lubricate ageing memories, and he had come upon someone who was able to direct them to what had been his parents' home. It was one of a row of identical dwellings, and there seemed to be some shadow of doubt as to which particular house deserved the honour. But in the end their informant seemed perfectly clear on the point and they knocked on the door.

The woman who answered listened sympathetically to the story and invited them in. She was herself a newcomer, she explained, and knew nothing at all about the former tenants, but if they could pick their way among her children – who seemed to be scattered everywhere – they were more than welcome. What with all this noise of children's laughter coupled with the proximity to the place of his own childhood, backed up by the numerous drams that had preceded it, the the American was becoming highly sentimental. So that when his attention was directed to the built-in bed in the kitchen where, it was to be presumed, the great event had occurred it proved too much and he broke down completely, shedding copious tears – to the considerable interest of the children.

Pulling himself together and thanking the woman for her courtesy he led the way out of the house of sacred memories.

The solicitor felt his client would definitely be the better for a little something to calm him down after this gruelling emotional experience, so he led the way back to the Black Bull where they sought the asylum of the Private Bar. They hadn't been there many minutes when the door was flung open and a little boy (one of the numerous brood from the birthplace) burst in breathlessly and announced, 'My mummy sent me to say ye've got it a' wrang. It should have been next door. You've been greetin' in the wrang hoose.'

Clearly I remember a Glasgow Church where during a vacancy they were enjoying the services of a most attractive and handsome young minister who had just completed a spell in a charge south of the border. The first Sunday there was a baptism he created quite a stir by awarding the child a most impressive and resounding 'holy kiss'. Scarcely was the service ended when the Session Clerk was approached by a lassie in the choir who wanted to know what you had to do to get christened again. The mention of a vacancy brings to mind this tale of a locum who learned the hard way the danger of figurative language in a situation where people are strictly literal – even in their puns!

The minister who had been acting as locum throughout the vacancy was taking his leave and was receiving many kindly acknowledgments from members of the congregation. Modestly brushing aside the compliments of one man he explained, 'I've just been a kind of stop-gap. You know how it is if you break a pane of glass in your window on a Saturday afternoon and can't get a joiner till Monday. You don't want the wind blowing through the house all weekend so you fix a piece of cardboard or some such thing to tide you over. That's what I've been – a stop-gap.'

'Na, na, minister, we're no' lettin' you away wi' that,' replied the well-satisfied member, 'you've been nae stop-gap, you've been a proper pane.'

For a final dig at the minister I would include this yarn, which is not so much an example of what could be as of what could not have been better put. The truth can be a very brutal thing, and it would appear that we are all sadist enough at heart to enjoy the sight of a man who has asked for it getting it fair on the chin.

The country minister had been ill. Unable to make his usual half-yearly round of a district with Communion Cards he had invoked the aid of the beadle. It was now John's third night and as usual he was reporting at the manse regarding his evening's activities. On the two previous nights he had been exuding a particularly healthy smell, but tonight he was emphatically the worse for the wear. The minister was remonstrating with him. 'John,' he said, 'for years I have visited these homes and never at any time have I been so much as invited to partake of alcoholic refreshment, and here you are, three nights running. Apart from being utterly ashamed of you I am at a loss to understand it.'

'Ah well,' said John, anxious to get to the root of the matter, 'it's like this, you're no' popular the way I am.'

I find it hard to believe that the following could not have been better put. A fairly stupid observation on the ostensible subject of discussion provides a remarkably shrewd assessment of a totally different subject, the result being quite funny.

The Provost of Invermuck, having occasion to be in London in pursuance of some of the weighty affairs of his ancient and historic royal burgh had found himself one afternoon in Savile Row. So impressed was he with the cut and style of some of the garments on show in the windows that he went in to one of the shops, selected a fine piece of material and had himself measured for a new suit. Some weeks later when the parcel arrived at Invermuck the Provost just couldn't wait to get into his grand London garments. Great was his sorrow, therefore, to find that the suit didn't even begin to fit him. The sleeves were halfway up his arms, he looked as if he had been moulded into the breeks, he was afraid to sneeze for fear of ripping the jacket up the back seam.

The whole affair was immediately sent back to London with an angry letter.

The tailor replied saying that he was at a loss to understand what could have happened. 'We have checked the garments,' he wrote, 'against the measurements that were most carefully taken on the occasion of your visit and we find that they correspond exactly. The only suggestion we can offer is that you must be a much bigger man at Invermuck than you are here in London.'

I don't think the hero of this last tale asked for it, but he certainly got it.

The aged, ill-fed donkey was putting up a gallant struggle in its attempt to haul the heavy-laden cart up a very steep hill, but it should have been apparent to all that the task was beyond its horse-power. The one person, seemingly, to whom it was not obvious was the stout Irishwoman in charge, for she sat proudly perched on top of the whole equipage shouting words of encouragement and belabouring the unfortunate beast with a stick.

With a view to shaming her into getting down from the cart a gentleman who had been passing got in alongside the donkey and pushed with might and main. The united effort proved adequate in due course to get the vehicle to the brow of the hill.

As the gentleman returned to the pavement, the grateful owner-driver acknowledged his contribution. 'Now that was rale kind of you, sor,' she said. 'Sure I knew the wan donkey would never make it.'

CHAPTER SIX

TURNING THE TABLES

SOMEWHERE IN THE MECHANISM of our being there is, I am convinced, a kind of spirit level, and we are so designed that we can have no peace of mind until we see things established on a basis of equity. Just as the sight of a picture on the wall hanging off the true can annoy us beyond endurance, so in other spheres too we like to see things restored to level. That, I imagine, is why we all find profound satisfacton at the sight of tables being turned in favour of justice, why we laugh so heartily when we see an adequate 'tit' following an aggressive 'tat', why we love to see the worm turn and put its tormentors to flight.

Why this basic sense of justice with its essentially moral foundation should have overtones is more than I can explain, but the fact is that many of our best stories have to do with the kind of situation where the simple man gives back an effective answer to his smart-alec opponent, where the victim who has been cleverly manoeuvred into a corner deftly extricates himself, where the man who has the last laugh has also the longest – and the heartiest – laugh. A soft answer turneth away wrath, the Scripture assures us; it's the apt answer that turneth away melancholy and maketh the heart glad.

A simple example of the kind of thing I have in mind is represented by the following tale from the days when railway stations enjoyed waiting-rooms with fires in their grates and when porters were around to see that the bye-laws were being duly observed. From which it will be seen that it is a story of considerable antiquity!

The man was seated contentedly in front of the fire in the waiting-room of a wayside railway station, his pipe going like the proverbial chimney. His peace was shattered by the entry of the porter who in stentorian tones demanded, 'Pit oot that pipe! Can ye no' read what it says there on the wa' – NO SMOKING?'

'Of course I can read fine,' replied the offender. 'But I canna be expected to do everything it says on your walls. Look at that,' pointing to another notice. 'How do you think I would look wearing a Cross-Your-Heart Bra?'

To some extent, I suppose, the element of fun in this arises from the ridiculous picture of the smoker draped in his bra, but what really evokes the laugh is the smartness and the aptness of the retort.

It's also from a country railway station in the days of long ago that the following exchange of courtesies comes.

The local train was puffing its way from one wayside station to the next and contriving to lose a lot of time in the process. At one of the stations an exasperated passenger was expressing his dissatisfaction in no uncertain terms to the guard who, however, was quite unimpressed. 'If that's how you feel,' he counselled, 'ye wad be faur better juist to get oot and walk the rest o' the way.' 'I had thought of that,' retorted the impatient traveller. 'Trouble is, my friends are not expecting me till the train.'

It's not perhaps surprising that in such a case the retort does not need to be logically convincing, so long as it is quick and devastating enough. There is, for example, what has always seemed to me the supreme masterpiece of irrelevance. The story, incidentally, has the added advantage, if it be an advantage, that it is true.

The minister was growing old, very old. He had been in his charge for longer than anyone cared to remember and there was increasing support for the view that a change would be to the benefit of all concerned. But the worthy divine showed no sign of taking any initiative. A small deputation was appointed to wait on him and tactfully suggest that he deserved a period of respite after so many years of arduous and unremitting toil.

The good man was not at all convinced. He expressed himself as grateful for their solicitude, but saw no reason why he should think of retiring. 'I still feel perfectly fit and able for my work,' he remonstrated. 'Has anyone suggested that I'm not doing my work adequately?' This set the deputation right back on its heels. 'Well,' ventured one of the group, 'some of the older folk have been saying that lately they haven't been hearing you too well.'

'I see,' said the minister. 'And tell me this, have they any reason to believe they would hear me any better were I to retire?'

As I say, the answer misses the charge by at least a mile – but you've got to admire its courageous confidence and you've got to laugh at it. If you have an idle moment you can even ask yourself how you would have challenged the answer, what would you have said by way of getting back into the attack.

There are cases where the defence is every bit as far from the mark as an adequate response to the charge without being nearly so clever and yet it may still be funny if the answer's quick enough. Indeed it is probably all the funnier for being logically so far from the mark.

As in the case of the Irishwoman at the customs post.

The cross-channel ferry had just berthed at Dover and the passengers were slowly making their way through Customs. The old Irishwoman declared she had nothing to declare, but the Customs official was minutely going through her baggage for all that.

Triumphantly he came up with a five-gill bottle. 'Aha,' said he, 'and what might this be?' 'O that,' she responded, 'that's a bottle of holy water that I'm taking home with me from Lourdes.' Unimpressed, the official withdrew the cork and applied the bottle to his his nose. 'Smells to me like whisky.' 'Give it to me here,' said the woman with an air of excitement. Applying it to her own nose she acclaimed, 'Glory be to God, an' if it isn't a miracle!'

On the other side there are cases where the logic is quite impeccable but they are not on that account either more or less funny than those where the premises will not support the conclusion. One is reminded of an old true tale.

In Glasgow in days gone by the Logic Class met immediately over the Greek class. One day the Greek professor was interrupted by plaster falling on his head as a result of a violent stamping of feet from above. Looking up he commented, 'I'm afraid our premises are inadequate to support Professor Jones's conclusions.'

But to return to our own case where the conclusion represents the outcome of perfect reasoning.

Auntie had just broken the bar of chocolate into two pieces slightly unequal in size as it happened. She offered the choice to her young nephew who without hesitation laid hold on the larger piece.

Anxious to instil habits of unselfishness Auntie explained, 'Now, Tommie, if it had been me who had been given the choice I should certainly have taken the smaller piece.'

'Well,' replied her very logical nephew, 'what are you girning about – you've got the smaller piece.'

A very dignified and self-important member of the club had just entered the premises when he was bumped into by a somewhat careless member of the staff who offered a rather curt and, in the member's view, inadequate, apology.

'Look, fellow, do you know who I am?' protested the outraged one.

'I regret to say, sir, that I do not,' replied the servitor. 'But if you will be so good as to take a seat for a few moments I shall make enquiry of one of the older club members and shall return and inform you.'

The old Glasgow tramcars which contributed so much to the humour of what was then the Second City (as well as to the convenient conveyance of its citizens), provide us with this tale of the sore harrassed passenger getting the score right at the expense of dignity and authority. The story was told in my hearing when I was a boy by an old lady who swore she had been there and had heard and seen it all. I'm inclined to believe her – it's far too incredible to be fictitious, apart altogether from the lady's honesty.

The passenger on the Saturday evening tram was at that stage of inebriation where he was at peace with the whole world and where his one ambition was that all men should be equally affectionately disposed towards him. So when he was approached by a very stout and pompous gentleman in uniform who wanted to see his ticket he was most anxious to oblige.

The ticket, however, proved elusive. One pocket was fumbled in after another. 'I've got a ticket a' right if I could juist mind wharra hell I put it.'

The other passengers were convulsed with mirth, a condition not shared by the man with the braid on his uniform. 'Look,' said that stout one in tones of stern exasperation, 'I'm going up to examine the tickets on the top deck. By the time I come back you can have done one of two things – either you can have found your ticket, or you can have bought a new ticket. If you haven't done either of these then you can jolly well get off and walk.'

'Terrible man that,' muttered the ticket-seeker still fumbling, 'terr'ble impatient man, to hear him goin' on you wad think I hadna got a ticket.' Just at that moment he struck oil and out of some inner recess of his clothing came the missing scrap of paper. 'I kent I had it a' the time,' he triumphantly proclaimed.

When, a minute or so later, the inspector waddled back, he seemed disappointed to be presented with a perfectly valid ticket, which he punched and handed back. As he was turning on his heel the inebriated one laid a hand on his shoulder, 'Wait a minute, Mister, there's something I want to tell you. You can do one of two things – either you can eat less, or else you can work more – an' if you cannie do one of these then you'll jolly well need to burst.'

Just to keep the balance straight there's this delightful story of the man in tramway uniform getting even with the ultra-smart passenger.

It was at the time when they brought out the first ticket-machines on the Glasgow trams. Until then tickets had been printed on long narrow strips of a card which varied in colour according to the fare paid, and bearing the names of all the fare-stages on the route, and which were punched by the conductor in such a way as to show the stage at which the tram had been boarded and that at which it had to be left. As has been said, in those days the conductor knew where he was, the passenger knew where he was, whereas on the bus today you're mighty lucky if the driver knows where he is.

The first models of the new machines were massive affairs, strapped around the conductor's shoulder and bearing a remarkable resemblance to the barrel organ used by the mendicant Italian musicians who, with their monkeys, were still occasionally to be found on the city streets. The similarity was increased by a series of buttons that had to be depressed to indicate the route, the fare paid, the stage boarded, and no doubt much further information. A handle was then turned and a sheet was torn off a roll of paper (almost the size of a toilet roll) with all the relevant data printed thereon. Certainly you could have been forgiven for expecting a tune as part of your reward.

One evening as the picture houses were skailing a very grand young gentleman accompanied by two young ladies boarded a green Dennistoun tram in the city centre. When he got his length the young man asked for 'three three-halfpenny ones.' The conductor got all the appropriate buttons duly depressed and was beginning to roll the presses when the young man remarked, 'That's a very fine organ you've got there, Conductor, but whatever's happened to your monkey?'

'It died,' was the instant reply. 'Was you lookin', for a job, like?'

Much more simply there's the tale of the ticket collector at the station barrier who was told by the rather up-stage commuter when asked for his ticket, 'My face is my ticket.' The reply was simple and to the point – 'OK, my orders are that I've to punch all tickets.'

There was a time in the twenties when the Glasgow tram was designed on the simple pattern of a gangway up the middle from stem to stern with wooden benches running the length of the vehicle on either side. It was as 'the caur' got busier that the conductor produced his stock phrase, 'Sit a little closer, please.' It was in such a car that the following interchange occurred.

The car was fairly busy, eleven people contriving to occupy all of the room designed for twelve on each side. A very stout gentleman came aboard and insisted on pushing into the minute space available, with the result that he was to all intents and purposes sitting on the lap of his neighbour, a man of the most modest proportions – indeed a skelf of a creature. With what breath he could muster the little man declared to the world in general, 'It would be a good idea if they charged by weight on these cars.' His oppressor patted him on the knee. 'You should be awfu' glad they don't. Nae driver wad ever stop for the likes o' you.'

In process of time and in the name of progress the city trams gave place to buses and men acting as conductors gave place to girls acting as conductresses. The popular name of 'clippie' was no doubt awarded in recognition of the lady's job of snipping bits out of tickets, but in most cases it could have been given with equal justice in respect of her ability to clip the wings of passengers suffering from an ambition to be smart. They have a phrase in some parts of Scotland when talking of someone with a blistering turn of phrase that she has a tongue that could clip cloots. Such was the heroine of this story from a bus stop in Johnstone.

A man with a whippet on a lead was standing at the head of the queue as the bus drew in to the kerb. His efforts to step on to the platform were, however, frustrated by the conductress who said, 'Sorry, I've a dug on already' – beckoning to two behind. The owner of the whippet was arguing vehemently.

Quite unmoved the lady took on the next two from the queue and rang the bell for the driver to proceed.

As the bus began to move off the whippet-owner gathered up all his sense of injustice and defeat, venting it in one final imprecation in which he indicated with some precision where she might put her bus, with particular reference to her jumper. The bus was now moving relentlessly away, but not so fast as to prevent the clippie shouting back, 'If you had had the sense to put your whippet there you would have got on.'

The minister features in this kind of joke – as he does in so much Scottish humour – and not surprisingly he is to be found at both the receiving and the delivering end of the *coup-de-grace*. You see the minister here, for instance, as the representative of theological authority being bested by the farmer who might normally have been expected not to excel in this department of human thinking.

The man of God was speaking very sternly to one of his farmers who had been living it up in the most reprehensible fashion. 'You know, John,' warned the divine, 'the devil goeth to and fro about the whole earth seeking whom he may destroy.' 'Dae ye tell me that, minister,' replied the man of the land. 'I was aye taught to believe that the devil was chained.'

The minister was too long in the theological tooth to be upset by a proposition so elementary as this. 'That is perfectly true, John,' he conceded, 'the devil is chained. But, you must understand, his chain covers the whole earth.'

'Weel of course if that's the way o't,' said John, exasperated as many better men have been before and since by the intricacies of such a theology, 'if that's the way o't the auld buggar micht as weel be louse.'

In passing it might be said at this stage that some part at least of the effectiveness of the tale lies in the earthy reference to the devil as 'the auld buggar.' This is to treat him almost as a member of the family. It is reminiscent, is it not, of Burns' attempt to find a suitable title for the gentleman – 'O thou whatever title suit thee, Auld Hornie, Satan, Nick, or Clootie.' Surely there is something very homely not to say deeply touching in Burns' invitation to the devil to 'tak a thocht an' men'. All this is completely in line with the tale of a minister of an earlier day of whom it is reported that he occasionally included in his prayer of intercession the petition, 'And, o Lord, gin it be Thy will, have mercy on the puir de'il.' Or an even friendlier and couthier note is struck in the case of the minister who in seeking a proper title for Auld Nick said he 'had nae doot 'devil' was correct enough, but for mysel' I like to ca' him de'il – it's mair freendly like.'

The reference to the devil in the story of the farmer from which this digression arose is 'freen'ly-like.' Nor can there be any doubt that expurgation at this point kills the story stone dead. You see the real point of the distinction between the minister and the farmer was that what for the one was a theological conception was for the other a warm (much too warm) reality.

I have myself occasionally heard the following well-known story told at kirk socials and the like with the offending expression exorcised. Those who told it thus seemed surprised at the poor response. They shouldn't have been, for they should have understood that a great part of the humour in the story lies in its acceptance of the de'il as part of the stuff of daily living. But to the story.

The Aberdeen-London express when it stopped at Perth had been boarded by, among others, a gentleman who clearly came straight from the door marked 'Refreshments'. By the perversity which attends such things he had elected to find a seat in a compartment whose only other occupant was a high ranking officer in the Salvation Army in all the splendour of his very grand uniform. He was deeply engrossed in a book and chose to take no notice of his new companion.

Not so the new arrival. From the moment he took his seat it was clear he was much interested in his fellow-traveller whom he studied from head to foot with meticulous care. They had travelled only a few miles when he leaned forward, tapped the officer on the knee and said, 'Sh-sh-shcuse me, but may I take the liberty of asking, are you in the Grenadier Guards?' 'O no, not at all,' said the other, continuing his earnest reading.

The detailed study having been resumed for some little time there came the second assault. 'Please don't think me inquish'tive, but I'm greatly interested in your uniform. Would I be right in thinking you're in the Marines?' 'I'm afraid no, not in the Marines.' And so back to the book.

A few miles later it became clear that a third attempt was to be made to find a suitable niche in the armed forces. This time it was the officer who took the initiative. Laying aside his book he said, 'My good man you appear to be much interested in this uniform of mine. Let me tell you that you are right in thinking I am a soldier, but a soldier in the Army of the Lord, dedicated to do battle with the devil. For five years I fought Satan in Inverness; for the past three years I have carried on the struggle in Aberdeen; and here I am on my way now to take up the battle afresh in Wolverhampton.' 'Thash fine, thash fine,' replied the tormentor. 'Keep it up. Juist you keep the auld buggar headin' south.'

To return to the minister in the squaring-of-the-account type of joke there are obvious entertainment possibilities in the picture of the man who ought to be turning the other cheek returning instead the cheeky answer. As in the tale, believed to be true, of the member who had no time for the law of the Kirk.

'Hello, minister, ye're the very man I wanted to see,' said a member, overtaking his minister on the street. 'I've been meanin' to come an' see you to arrange for you to come to the hoose some night and baptise oor new wean.'

Said the minister, 'I'm sorry to hear that yor wife's not well.'

'Wha telt ye that? The wife's fine an' so's the wean.'

'In that case,' said the minister, 'you'll all come to church and we'll have the baptism properly during the morning service.'

'Naw, naw,' said the father, 'I'm no' for havin' it on a Sunday. You'll juist come along to the hoose and have it quietly there.'

The minister stuck to his guns, insisting that except in the case of illness baptism must necessarily be in Church in face of the congregation. Father was equally adamant he wasn't having it that way. Who said it had to be in Church anyway. Because, explained the minister, that is the law of the Church of Scotland.

'I don't give a damn for the law of the Church of Scotland,' responded the member who went on to say that he would lift his lines and go elsewhere.

By this time they were close to the Manse, so the minister suggested that if the dissatisfied customer would come in for a minute he would write out his disjunction certificate there and then – which he did.

It was only when the man had got to his own house that he had an opportunity of studying the Certificate of Transference and of discovering what it said – 'This is to certify that Mr John Black leaves the congregation of St Mungo's because he doesn't give a damn for the law of the Church of Scotland.'

It is, I believe, even better when the simple man of God can be seen to be scoring at the expense of the smart-alec man-of-the-world – particularly if the latter happens to be a none too civil civil servant. The question arose many years ago over the issue of who should dispose of a body.

It was back in the old days when ministers were ministers and manses were manses and never the twain did part. One morning the country minister who is the hero of our tale went into his garden to stroll and to meditate. He hadn't progressed far in either pursuit when he was abruptly halted by the sight of a deceased donkey lying in his rose-bed. It was immediately apparent to him that a troop of tinkers who had been in the village the day before had had the beast die on their hands and having contrived to get the body over the manse wall had gone upon their way.

The minister returned to his study where he penned a letter to the County Sanitary Inspector narrating the circumstances and ending by calling upon the official to take immediate steps to have the offending body disposed of.

The Inspector was a man of some ingenuity, so he replied acknowledging the letter and noting the situation, but going on to say that in his understanding the minister was in receipt of a stipend made up of certain tiends which in turn imposed specific obligations, one of these being 'a responsibility to bury the dead of the parish.' Before subscribing himself 'Your Obedient Servant' he went on to make the suggestion that the minister should do just that.

The minister was not so easily vanquished. He replied, agreeing that he was in receipt of tiends and that this in turn involved obligations. The specific responsibility here in question, he went on to explain, was that he conduct a suitable service at all interments within the parish. 'The responsibility for arrangng the actual physical burial, however, rests with the next-of-kin, and I have therefore to repeat the requirement in my earlier letter.'

It would be extremely difficult in this next tale to say who scored at the expense of whom, but it does represent a delightful illustration of how easily the simple countryman can fill the role of philosopher.

The kirk was a tiny affair near the head of a lonely glen; the congregation were few in number, all of them having far to travel; the Sunday was miserable and bleak beyond description; the solitary farmer sat hopefully in his pew; but as time passed it became obvious that he was to be the only worshipper. The minister slipped into the church and sat down beside his 'congregation.'

'Bob,' he said, 'I'm in a bit of a dilemma. I'm all prepared to take a service and feel that I ought to do so. On the other hand it could be a bit embarrassing for you sitting here all by yourself. What do you think I ought to do?'

'Weel, minister, as I see it it's like this,' Robert replied without hesitation, 'suppose I go oot wi' a bag o' cake to feed the stirks. I go to the troughs an' I gi'e a bit whustle. If there was only wan stirk cam' in answer to my whustle I wouldna walk awa' an' leave her hungry – I would feed her.'

'How right you are, Bob. I stand reproved.' Away went the minister, appearing a few minutes later in the pulpit fully robed. And the service proceeded through all its steps as to a full house.

The benediction having been pronounced and the minister having changed his robes for his outdoor wear he joined Bob on the road. For a while they walked in silence and then Bob remarked, 'Ye mind, minister, I said that suppose only wan stirk cam furrit for her cake I wad feed her?' 'I do indeed,' said the minister, 'I won't quickly forget that lesson. Your point was so admirably taken.'

'Ay but here, minister,' Bob protested,' I never said I wad gi'e her the whole bagfu'.'

Is not there something wondrously satisfying in the punch-line of the story of the wet-blanket barber? We've all known people of his type – only trouble is we're not usually in a position to deal with them so faithfully.

The man was having his hair cut. 'And where,' enquired the barber, 'are you going for your holiday this year?' The customer replied that he and his wife were thinking of Italy. 'Oh, I don't know I would advise you to go to Italy, sir. An awful lot of my customers are saying Italy's not what once it was. One man who comes in here tells me he used to go every year, but he's not going back – ever.'

After a few more minutes of clipping the barber took up the lament afresh and on learning it was Rome that was in view his sympathy knew no bounds. 'They all tell me that Rome's really terrible. You're not even safe to go out after dark.' In lugubrious tones he added, 'I would think twice before going to Rome.'

Again a period of silent clipping, and then a question as to which hotel in Rome. The answer to this left him completely devastated. 'I've a man who comes in here who went to that hotel last year and he said he wouldn't go back if they invited him free of charge – they couldn't eat the food, their bedroom was no more than clean, they couldn't sleep at night for the noise from the bar.'

It was some months later that the man appeared in the same shop. 'Hello, sir,' said the barber. 'You're the man who was going to Rome for your holiday. How did you get on?'

'It's like this,' replied the customer, 'we had the best holiday we've ever had in our life – the hotel was excellent, the food was good, the price was reasonable. We went everywhere, we saw everything. You know, we even had an audience with the Pope.'

'Do you tell me that,' said the incredulous barber, pausing in his clipping the better to hear the details. 'Indeed we had,' said his client, 'and when the audience was over I bent down and the Pope laid his hand on my head, and do you know what he said – he speaks perfect English, you know?'

'What did he say?' breathlessly enquired the man with the shears.

He said, 'My God, who cut your hair?'

In its couthie, cannie, country way the tale of the ploughman who had to get a character reference has the ring of truth to it and exemplifies the same tit-for-tat principle.

It was way back in the days of the feeing-fair when farm workers were engaged for six months at a time and were fee-ed in the market-place by the striking of hands and the passing of a half-crown as arles in token of their engagement.

A farmer had made contact with what seemed a likely ploughman. Terms had been discussed in some detail and the point had been reached when both sides seemed close enough to conclude a bargain. The farmer, however, was reticent because the servant did not have a character reference. 'I wad have liked it better if ye had had a "character",' he insisted. 'I ay like to see a "character" afore I engage a man.'

'I tell you what,' said the prospective servant. 'I was two years wi' Willie Broon oot at The Mains. It wouldna take me a' that long to run doon there on my bike, and he wad gi'e me a character, I'm sure.' The arrangement commended itself, the farmer undertook to hang around till his return and if the character was up to standard they could strike hands and make it a bargain.

It was later – a very long time later – that the farmer caught sight of his ploughman-elect. 'Here you,' he protested, 'I thocht you were oot at The Mains getting your "character". What have you been dae'in a' this time?'

'It was like this,' explained the ploughman, 'I went to The Mains to get my character an' I got yours instead – an' I'm no' comin'.'

And again though this time it's a tale of city folk, there is the same couthie quality in the rejoinder that makes the yarn fall inevitably into the same group. Here again the complainer is left without a possible come-back.

They were an ageing Glasgow couple and they were having guests in for supper. While they were busy setting the table the lady said to her better half, 'An' when we get them a' sat doon at the table I'll gi'e you a nod an' that'll be your cue to say grace. An' you'd better get busy right awa' an' mak' up yer mind what you're goin' to say. An' speak oot nice an' clear and don't juist sit there an' mum'le the way you usually do.'

The guests had been and had supped and had gone home and the subsequent dish-washing was in progress, the while the evening's doings were made the subject of a post-mortem. 'And anither thing,' pursued said the lady, 'for all I warned you aforehand aboot the grace and to ha'e something ready ye juist sat there at the head o' the table an' girned awa' under yer breath. I'm sure not one of the guests could make oot a single word you were sayin'.'

Which elicited the somewhat truculent – if logically impeccable – reply, 'I wasna' speakin' to them.'

Talking of grace inspires a parenthetical reference to the Bishop who was attending a public dinner and was invited by the chairman to say grace. 'I should rather not,' he said. 'Frankly I'd be happier to think God didn't know I was here.'

A much more sophisticated position is displayed in the next couple of tales which strictly do not belong here since they represent the smart guy stealing a march on authority rather than getting the account put straight. The element of amusement arising from the slickness of the reaction is, however, the same.

First of all there is the American go-getter who if he can't 'getter' the one way will certainly 'getter' the other!

The American business magnate had got himself involved in some litigation in Scotland and his case was due to come before the Court of Session. A few days in advance of the hearing a consultation was being held with counsel and solicitors. His prospects, he was assured, were far from bright. As the meeting was drawing to a close he asked, 'This Lord Abermuchty who, you say, is to be on the bench, where does he reside?' A number in Moray Place was mentioned. 'But why do you want his address?' 'O I just thought I might send him a case of whisky and a few good cigars.'

Needless to say, consternation broke loose. Uncle Sam's nephew was warned that his hopes of success were slender enough already, that however this kind of thing might pass in Illinois it would be suicidal here, that in Scotland any kind of approach to the bench could be counted on to finish your chances, and so on. The litigant thanked them for the information and pursued the subject no further.

In due course the case was called and to the amazement of all concerned – except the American – not only was judgment given in his favour but His Lordship went out of his way to pass some bitterly scathing comments upon the other party to the action.

Later the victorious one was being congratulated by counsel. 'Yes,' he replied, 'it was well worth the price of the whisky and the cigars.' 'Good heavens, you didn't send him those after all we said to you in warning,' gasped the incredulous advocate. 'Of course I sent them to him, but thanks to your warning I took the precaution of seeing the card had the other fella's name on it.'

It would be difficult to outdo the tactics of the no less slick city pub-crawler who got himself a free dram – two in fact.

The stranger in the pub just stood at the bar. After he had been there for a minute or two without showing any sign of giving an order the publican enquired, 'Well, my friend, and what is your pleasure?' 'Thank you very much,' said the stranger, 'I'll have a Black and White – an' no' too much water.'

The whisky was laid on the counter. The stranger having himself added the 'no' too much water' began to drink, totally ignoring the publican's demand, 'That'll be sixty-five pence.' The demand was repeated. 'Look here,' said the stranger, 'I'm no' owing you anything. I never ordered a drink. It was when you, out of the goodness of your heart, insisted that I must have something that I said I would take a Black and White.'

The argument continued for a little. 'OK,' said the barman, 'you win. Fine I know your kind. You're the smart guy that gets a drink for nothing. Well, go on and drink up and get out of that door. Ay, and see and enjoy your drink for it's the last you'll get here, free or otherwise. Just you so much as show your miserable face round that door and you'll be back out on the street so fast you'll wonder what hit you.' Quite unperturbed the stranger went on enjoying his whisky in leisurely fashion. He then departed wishing his host a hearty goodnight.

It was the very next day that he reappeared, accompanied by a friend. Immediately he was assailed with the demand to get out. 'What do you mean get out?' he innocently enquired.

'You're the smart guy that was in here last night and I warned you what would happen if ever I saw your dirty face in here again. And you've got the effrontery to be back the very next day.'

'Last night you say this happened?' diligently pursued the stranger. 'If it happened last night it couldna have been me, for I was workin' late till long after closin' time. Isn't that right, Willie,' turning to his friend for corroboration of his alibi.

'That's right,' confirmed his friend. 'It couldna have been Bob here, for I was workin' alongside o' him in the factory till near midnicht, an' he never left the place a' that time. Whoever it was that done you it couldna have been Bob.'

'Well,' said the publican his confidence in his power of identification shaken, 'if it wasn't you, you must have a double.'

'Oh thank you very much,' said the stranger, 'juist mak' that a Black an' White tae – an' no' too much water.'

I should like to end this chapter with a very entertaining story which depends to no small extent upon the telling. It belongs to this group, I contend, because it shows there is another side to getting even – that of paying the debt incurred, or, if you will, of singing for your supper. You know, incidentally, the wisecrack that supper comes before singing – but only in an Irish dictionary. In the circumstances outlined below the singing was done in a most professional and effective fashion. But then, you see, the man was a professional.

A friend of mine tells the story that one day, returning to Glasgow from a business trip in the north-east corner of Scotland he was flagged down by a man seeking a lift – to Glasgow.

Glad of any company on a long trip my friend welcomed the stranger aboard and soon they fell into conversation about this and that. It appeared that the stranger had just completed a spell as a guest of Her Majesty in an institution which she maintains at Peterhead, of which it can be said that even if it is not a five-star hotel it costs a good deal more to keep you there for a week than it would at a five-star hotel.

He explained that he graduated to this height – or depth as you care to call it – by easy stages. He had been the child of a broken home – 'never had a proper chance, sir' – and had early fallen into habits of truancy, which had proved indescribably dull unless enlivened by excursions into shop-lifting and pocket-picking. Success in these pursuits led him to turn his attention to breaking and entering and other more sophisticated forms of self-help.

The incident which led to his recent period of incarceration had, however, all been due to a misunderstanding. One warm summer's day he had gone into a bank to ask for change of a pound, and while there he had very civilly agreed to hold a sawn-off shot-gun for one of the other customers who wished to speak to the cashier. The situation had been complicated and his own position prejudiced by the fact that the day having been unusually warm he had pulled a silk stocking over his face to protect him from the attention of the midges.

It would appear that the bank manager, who was a very nervous man, had thought that a raid was in progress and had called in the police. Not all the forensic skills of senior and junior counsel – kindly provided by legal aid – succeeded in persuading a heavily prejudiced jury of the young man's bona fides. Hence his unmerited sojourn in the north.

With all this pleasant chatter the miles were slipping by unheeded and they were passing through the town of Auchterarder when they were overtaken and waved into the side of the road. A man in blue appeared at the window asking whether my friend was aware that at various points within this built-up area he had been driving at speeds in excess of the statutory thirty miles an hour. My friend replied that he was not aware of this but that he was open to conviction. Whereupon the man in blue produced a note-book in which he entered all sorts of particulars about vehicle and driver.

His next concern was to enquire whether my friend would care to say anything that would be written down and used in evidence against him – as if they hadn't enough of that already! He seemed a trifle disappointed when my friend declined, so buttoning away his book he had a further walk around and careful inspection of the car and its contents, and then, telling his victim that he would be hearing from the procurator-fiscal in due course, he bade them *bon voyage* in the kindly tones the police reserve for those who have been assisting them with their enquiries.

The remainder of the journey, needless to say, passed on a much lower key and when they had arrived at the outskirts of the city the 'fare' indicated a point that he said would suit him admirably – it was within easy scaling distance of Barlinnie. As he got out of the car he turned to my friend and said, 'As I telt ye I'm fresh oot the jile and I've nae money to pay for the lift. But,' he added casually, producing a book from his pocket, if that polisman's note-book's ony use to you you're welcome to it.'

Singing for his supper – ay indeed; though for myself I would rather call the story No Charge for the Lift.

CHAPTER SEVEN

GETTING IN DEEPER

UNLESS YOU ARE A HIGHLY-SKILLED MECHANIC, running repairs to your car are both difficult and dangerous to execute – you're much better to stop the engine and consider carefully what you are about. I doubt if there is any field of human activity where this is truer than in that of communication. To try to amend a thought while engaged in expressing it demands a degree of expertise that few of us possess. And if you happen to be as clever as that you should have got it right first time round.

I have always maintained that if in the course of conversation you make a 'floater' the wise thing to do is to leave it floating and hurry on. If you succeed in doing this fast enough the slickness of the voice may deceive the ear, your hearer may not pick up the mistake at all, or, if he does, he may conclude you haven't noticed it, let alone that you had intended it. In either case the matter will be quickly forgotten. If, on the other hand, you, pause to retract and apologise you merely draw attention to what should have been allowed to pass.

In that connection it's perhaps worth saying that people can say the most outrageous things quite unintentionally and without realising afterwards what they have done. I remember a minister in the Presbytery of Paisley who, in an impassioned address one night, said he thought the members of the Business Committee should put their heads together and form a round table. He was baffled to understand the howls of merriment that ensued.

Obviously he hadn't heard the classic one about the do-it-yourself man who had made a chest of drawers out of his own head and had enough wood over to make a desk.

The one thing you must certainly never do is to try and extricate yourself. That way you invariably get in deeper, that way you can count on turning a trifling embarrassment into a major disaster. For the onlooker it can be outrageously funny, but not so for the perpetrator. The best example of what I have here in mind is this magnificent tale.

In the course of a very splendid dinner a gentleman whispered to his lady partner, 'Do you happen to know who that particularly ugly woman is sitting to the right of the chairman?'

'That,' replied the lady in distinctly frigid tones, ' is Miss Blank, who happens to be my sister.'

'Dear me,' flustered her partner, 'but how terribly stupid of me. Of course I should have known. If only I had stopped to think I would have seen the family resemblance.'

After an effort of that kind, suicide must seem a kindly way out. Of a piece with that, though not nearly so bad is the sad story of the society hostess who got it all wrong with the Bishop – just when she was so anxious to get it all right.

The at-home was in full swing when the Bishop arrived. The salon was packed with the most distinguished people, each with a glass in hand. A warm welcome was extended to His Grace and quickly he was in conversation with this one and that, but no one offered him anything to drink. The servitors who were milling around with trays seemed to be studiously avoiding catching his eye.

After a while he found himself in conversation with Madame. 'I wonder,' he said to her, 'if I might have something to drink.' 'Oh,' she replied in some confusion. 'You see I had somehow got it into my head that you didn't take anything – indeed that you were President or something of the Total Abstainer Union.'

'Dear me, no,' said His Grace, 'there is no one enjoys a glass more than I do – in strict moderation, of course. It may be, you know,' he went on, 'that confusion has arisen because I happen to be chairman of the Anti-Vice League in the diocese.'

'But of course that's what it is,' said his hostess. 'Stupid me. I've got it mixed up as usual. I was sure there was something I must remember not to offer you.'

Then there was the kirk elder whose efforts to explain away the unfortunate idiosyncracies of the village simpleton led to a situation where he was himself acting very much in that capacity.

It was less than a month after he had been inducted to the parish that the minister was one day walking down the street when he became conscious of being followed at a respectful distance by a young fellow obviously of low mentality who chanted in dreary tones. 'Ye canna preach for toffee, ye canna preach for toffee.' This was going on to the point of monotony, so the minister took shelter by turning into a shop. The shopkeeper being one of his elders he told him of his experience, hastening to add that he was not in the least offended but only curious to know more about who the young chap was.

'Oh that,' explained the elder, 'that would be Daft Wull. Everybody hereabouts kens Daft Wull. He's no' 'a there, of course, twa-three coppers short of the shillin.' Then he added, 'But ye mustna worry aboot what Wull says. He's no really responsible – he juist goes aboot repeatin' whatever he hears.'

And to round off this little section there is the story of the parrot that had still to be instructed in the art of swearing, but that looked like beginning its tuition quite soon.

The hardy salt was trying to sell a parrot to a most dignified maiden lady. It was clear that he would have been much more at home singing the chorus of 'Yo, ho, ho, and a bottle of rum' than trading in the kind of market in which he was presently engaged. Question relentlessly followed question.

'Does he swear?' she enquired apprehensively. 'Not at all, madam, but it wouldn't take long in your company before he would learn.'

Talking of parrots reminds me of another tale and leads me to say that it is possible to get in deeper as a result of our actions no less than of our words, as is illustrated in this tale of the parrot that had learned to swear.

The two Miss Prims had acquired a parrot the clarity of whose diction was their pride and joy. The only dark cloud on their horizon was that on occasion Polly's language left a good deal to be desired if little to be imagined. One evening, glancing round the edge of the lace curtain Miss Euphemia spied the minister coming up the drive. 'For goodness sake Penelope, be quick and put the cover over Polly's cage while I go and open the door for Mr Bloggs. Would it not be dreadful if we had any bad language while he's here.'

Miss Penelope did as requested. Which presumably explains why as Miss Euphemia ushered the man of the cloth into the sitting-room, though no speaker was to be seen, a disgruntled voice was to be clearly heard saying, 'Hellova short day, this!'

One of the most embarrassing experiences of my own professional life is associated with the case of a man who insisted on getting in deeper.

The occasion was a social gathering to welcome a new minister. The kirk was packed with people and the programme was packed with items. There is a widespread idea that no such event is complete unless every minister who neighbours on the parish and every ministerial friend of the new arrival is invited to make a five-minute contribution. It is further expected that these contributions shall be vastly entertaining. To the average induction-social-goers that seems little enough to expect.

Now to make inside five minutes a speech that will be to any degree relevant, meaningful and funny is a task demanding considerable skill and experience, not to mention some native ability as a wit. The result is only too often that some silly stories that have no conceivable connnection with the occasion are rather badly told to the accompaniment of some highly processed artificial laughter that would do credit to a television audience.

On the evening of which I speak we had reached that point in the programme when Mr West the longest-serving minister in the town was to 'offer greetings'. Now Mr West was an excellent parish minister, he was the kindliest of neighbours, he was a fine Christian gentleman, but as an *ex tempore* speaker he rambled shockingly and as a story-teller he flopped miserably. So he began with a joke. I've forgotten now what it was meant to be, but it was one of that silly kind of blether that gains any point it has by scoring off one of the other denominations. It didn't matter what denomination you chose to be the fall-guy, so Mr West had to pick on the Baptists and that in spite of the fact that the only other denomination represented on the platform was the local Baptist minister, a very touchy young man. As Mr West reached the denouement of his tale the penny dropped in his own mind – others of us had seen it coming from afar. Suddenly he realised where he was going and he tried to draw back, the only result being that he botched the joke (such as it was) and underlined the result to the Baptists (so far as there was one). Since it was a joke that had got him into this mess he decided apparently that a second joke would get him out of it. All that his second effort at being witty did was to underscore further the unfortunate reference to the Baptists. Having, as it were, accidentally splashed some mud he now proceeded to smear it over his victim. Even to Mr West's none too sensitive consciousness it was now apparent that all was not well so – believe it or not – he launched out on a third attempt to remedy the situation with yet another stupid irrelevent and ill-timed joke. By this time, mercifully, the congregation had recovered from their embarrassment and were convulsed with mirth – not at the jokes in particular but at the situation in general. With a gentle pulling of his coat tails and in the good spirits now prevailing Mr West resumed his seat to the intense relief of me at least and I happened to be in the chair.

As I said at the outset, if you make a floater, pretend you haven't seen it and hurry on. If, for example, you greet a lady, 'Oh, it's you Mrs Dowdy, I didn't recognise you at first you're looking so smart,' then certainly you haven't covered yourself with glory. But the lady may have accepted the compliment and not noticed the implications. She won't be happy for long if you hurry on to add, 'I don't mean that you're not always well-dressed but only that today you happen to be looking very smart.'

If you say to a vocalist who has just been entertaining the company that he should have his voice trained, leave him to draw whatever implications he likes – don't under any circumstances start explaining what you didn't mean, for the only result of that will be to make abominably clear what you did mean!

There is a very sound rule given to those who sit examinations that they should confine themselves strictly to answering the questions asked, neither more or less. It is indeed good advice and worthy to be followed. The hero of the following story must surely never have heard the warning or – perhaps more likely – he had decided that he knew better.

The sanctified plumber had made repeated efforts to enter the theological college with a view to training for the ministry, but nothing had come of his perseverance for he could never get past the entrance examination in Scripture Knowledge. Year after year he presented himself and year after year he failed lamentably.

After a time the examiners put their heads together to devise a scheme whereby he could be allowed through – such perseverance, they felt, deserved some recognition, and once in the College he would be better acquainted with the Bible anyway. So that when next he presented himself he was told that this year he was to have an oral instead of the usual written examination. There would be one question. He was to take his time and think carefully before answering it. Name any one of the Kings of Israel. He accepted their advice about taking plenty of time and thinking carefully. At last, very hesitantly he ventured, 'Saul'.

Splendid, Mr Geyser, that is all we want to ask you. You may go now. The results will be published tomorrow.

Elated with his success he turned half-way out of the door and added, 'He was also called "Paul".'

Mention of the Kings of Israel leads one to interject the tale of the divinity student who in preparing for an examination had been assured he had better swot up on the Kings of Israel for inevitably there would be a question on that subject. Imagine his horror on seeing the paper and finding that the examiners had devised a new question: Write a note on the influence exerted by the prophets of Israel. But he was equal to the occasion. 'The prophets exerted a considerable influence on the history of Israel. They were, however, much overshadowed by the Kings of Israel . . .' And so the needle was got into the proper groove or so the examinee hoped.

To return, though, to the consideration of ways in which you can get yourself into trouble at oral examinations.

When Mr Flopp, student in law, presented himself for the oral part of the examination in Evidence and Procedure he was told by the professor that his mark in the written paper had been so low it was not proposed to give him an oral. 'But,' he protested, 'I must have an oral. The ordnance says so.' 'Yes, yes Mr Flopp, but there's no point wasting your time and ours when, supposing you got a hundred per cent you still wouldn't pass.'

Mr Flopp was not satisfied. 'Look,' he said, 'the ordnance lays it down that every candidate is to be examined both by written paper and by oral interrogation. I demand my oral. If I don't get it I'll raise an action in court.'

'And tell me Mr Flopp what kind of action will you raise?' 'I don't know off-hand, but I'll find out.'

'Very good, Mr Flopp you have now had your oral examination and I regret to tell you that you have failed.'

Probably these stories about orals do not conform strictly to the title of this chapter but more aptly to one entitled Digging One's Own Grave. Which reminds me of the yarn about the man who contrived to do just that – three times over – and in a graveyard at that.

The Englishman was on holiday in a little Scottish village. Out for a stroll early one morning and passing the graveyard he realised that a grave was being dug. Wandering into the kirkyard he remarked to the grave-digger, who by this time was down so far that only his head could be seen from ground level, 'It's quiet down here.' He received the reply, 'It's quieter still doon here.' He tried again, 'I'm sure people must like being buried in this lovely spot,' which elicited the response, 'I've never heard ony o' them complainin'.' The visitor made one last heroic effort, 'Tell me,' he said, 'do people die often in these parts?' to which came the laconic reply, 'Juist the wance.'

And on that note I think we should bury the whole affair.

CHAPTER EIGHT

THE DIRTY CRACK

I HAVE CHOSEN THIS TITLE deliberately for I want to illustrate the resort to humour for purposes that are far from kindly. A joke can be blunt, a smart riposte can be cutting, fun can be brutal. Humour generally speaking is a kindly, gentle thing and the people about whom we make jokes are usually the people we like and respect, even if we smile at their foibles.

Derision, however, is not a kindly thing, having in its composition some of the acid of cynicism. And humour can provide the vehicle for derisive comment. The comment will not normally be made in so many words, but the hint is given and the conclusion inescapable. In fact it is here precisely that the fun comes in - not in what is said but in what is left to be supplied by the hearer.

The following is a good example of what I have in mind.

The lady was upbraiding her husband in the matter of infidelity on his part of which she had become aware. He appeared remarkably unimpressed with either harsh words or bitter tears. So she tried an appeal to his sense of fairness: 'What would you do,' she enquired, 'if you came home one night and found me in bed with another man – just what would you do?'

'What wad I do?' he retorted. 'Well I'll tell you the first thing I wad dae. I wad take his white stick an' break it ower his back.'

Strictly speaking there is not, I am sure, anything really funny about that story. Yet it can be counted on to produce a smile – albeit a wry smile – in any average male audience. It all turns on that one word 'white'. Omit that and you don't have a funny story at all. It's the subtle allusion to the lady's homely appearance as witnessed by the poor sight of her paramour, a fact witnessed in turn by the white stick – it's all these unexpressed stages in the argument that enable it to provoke a smile – if not on the lady's face.

You need to know Glasgow with its bitter Rangers–Celtic rivalry if you are to be able to supply the missing link in the thinking of this nasty tale.

The young husband was getting himself togged out in his blue and white jersey, muffler, tammy and other Rangers paraphernalia preparatory to setting forth for the fitba', leaving the wife at home with the weans.

'You know, Willie, I sometimes think you've got to love thae Rangers mair than you love me.'

To which he ungallantly responded, 'Don't you kid yoursel' Maggie, there are times when I love Celtic mair than I love you.'

There's mighty little real humour there – it's just a dirty crack with nothing to redeem it. It's really a shame so much as to smile at the poor lassie's humiliation. For all that the story has produced many a roar of laughter in its time.

The late Professor Herbert J Paton when he was in the Chair of Logic at Glasgow University in the 'thirties had an Ordinary Class of over five hundred students. For obvious reasons the class met normally in two sections, but on the final day of term it met as one for purposes of prize-giving and leave-taking. Vividly I recall the occasion in my own year.

We were packed into the class-room, all five hundred of us, like the proverbial sardines, and the professor was bidding us (or at least a good few of us) farewell. The prizes had been distributed and he was coming to the end of an intensely interesting talk on 'Logic and Living'.

'And now,' he concluded in his slow, deliberate Oxford accent, 'nothing remains for me but to wish you one and all the very best of luck in the forthcoming degree examinations . . .' Tumultuous applause interrupted him at this point, clapping, cheering, foot-stamping, cat-calling, whistling, the lot.

He availed himself of the interruption to gather together his papers in one hand, to take his mortar-board in the other, and to move back across the platform towards the door leading to his side-room. Then as the din subsided he quietly finished his sentence, '. . . for some of you will most certainly need it.'

That crack was most certainly 'dirty' enough in all conscience. Yet it was extremely funny and produced howls of merriment – even if it should be added that many of us were, in the popular phrase, laughing on the wrong side of our faces. The entertaining aspect in a crack of this kind is the way in which you are lifted up and then so suddenly and unexpectedly let down. And there was also, of course, the perfect timing.

The same kind of thing is even more brutally exemplified in the following yarn where the crack is surely as cold as it is dirty – and, what is worse, not really deserved.

The day was as miserable a day a could be – cold, wet, windy. From earliest light bleats of sleet had swept across the kirkyard on the edge of the hill. As the company huddled round an open grave the minister hurried through the committal service. The benediction pronounced, the mourners quickly made their way to the shelter of the cars. Only the chief mourner and the grave digger were left standing.

'A terrible day to have to open a grave,' remarked the next-of-kin of the deceased.' 'It was a' that, sir.' 'You must be soaked to the skin.' 'I am that richt enough.' 'You look real cold at the moment.' 'I'm frozen to the bone, sir.'

'Tell me, do you take a dram?' 'I would never say "No" to the offer of a dram – especially on a day like this.'

'Well,' pointing down into the grave, juist you take that for a warning an' learn to say "No". He was awfu' fond o' a dram tae an' couldna say "No", an' ye see whaur it's brought him, a man as young as yoursel'.'

To return to our first story of the man with the white stick where the humour lies in the hint of an argument, in the stages of the reasoning left to be supplied by the hearer, it would surely be hard to surpass the following masterpiece, where the boarder scores off the landlady in such neat and nasty fashion. For when all's said and done there's no fairer game than the proprietrix of the holiday-resort boarding-house. Nothing can be too nasty for one so mean, particularly as she has the last laugh – she tenders the bill.

The family were on holiday and had booked into a modest boarding-house for bed and breakfast. The quality of the breakfast was good enough, but the quantity left a lot to be desired. Each boarder was issued with a plate carrying one solitary rasher of bacon and an egg that might well have been laid by a pigeon. This was followed by a second plate on which was a single slice of bread, and, to assist in its digestion a tiny morsel of butter.

After three days of this one of the guests approached the hostess – not an easy undertaking, she being so far from approachable – with the suggestion that the morning provision might be increased. When she asked for specific proposals his courage was already waning and the best he could get round to was 'a little jam or something with their bread.'

The lady promised to give the matter her most sympathetic consideration.

Next morning the serving of the enhanced breakfast was anxiously awaited.Everything was exactly as before till they came to the bread course. This time alongside the morsel of butter there was just enough suggestion of honey to make the edge of the plate sticky. As she put down the helping thus adorned, the hostess looked defiantly in the direction of the trouble-maker.

'Ah, Miss M'Meanie,' he said happily, 'I see you keep a bee.'

In the same class though very different in content falls the story of the soldier sharing a compartment on the train.

It was evident enough that while awaiting the arrival of the train the soldier had been celebrating. To anyone accustomed to the changing pattern produced under the influence of alcohol it was clear that our hero had reached the stage characterised by a spirit of good will towards all of God's creatures, that stage when he was convinced that everyone was his friend, and when he wanted them each to know just how highly he thought of them. Naturally he expected a little love and understanding in return. It was perhaps unfortunate that he found himself sharing a compartment with a pariculary frigid lady who made it clear she was not impressed by his spirit of bonhomie and that she had no intention of reciproca-ting. His every attempt at conversation was either ignored completely or elicited a chilly and unsympathetic rejoinder. Still he persisted until she put down her paper and said, 'My man, I have no intention of entering into a conversation with you. You are drunk, you are abominably drunk, you are disgustingly drunk.'

The message got through and the journey proceeded in silence. A couple of stations further along the line the warrier got out, and with the door still open in his hand he fired his parting shot. 'Madam,' he said, 'you are ugly, you are abominably ugly, you are disgustingly ugly.' And then as he was about to bang the door shut he added, 'An' what's more, I'll be sober by the morning.'

At the end of the line of undeveloped argument in the following tale there is something very sharply cutting, even if also very richly deserved. How often have I wished I could have produced something half as good when placed in a similar situation.

Two men were standing at a street corner deeply engrossed in conversation when they were interrupted by a passer-by who crashed in with the question, 'Is there a toilet anywhere around here?'

Said one of them, 'If you go along as far as the next corner, turn to your left and walk on for about fifty yards you will see a stair leading down and over the entrance a notice which reads 'Gentlemen'. Just you ignore that and go on down.'

On the other hand this next tale has just that shade of kindliness that takes away some of the sting. Though I shouldn't have liked to be at the receiving end.

A wide representation of the local community was gathered in the town hall, for there had arisen an issue of considerable local interest that demanded to be discussed. The little burgh boasted a single-page news-sheet that appeared once a week and of which one of the local residents was the printer, the editor, the publisher, the advertising manager and the sole director. In virtue of this he not unnaturally saw himself as a figure of some light and leading in the community. They had reached a stage in the evening's proceedings when this individual felt inspired to intervene and to present the point of view of the media – as he felt peculiarly qualified to do. Having cleared his throat rather ostentatiously he began, 'We editors . . .'

Before he could proceed any further a voice from the back of the hall interjected, 'Ay, awfu' wee.'

An incident like the undernoted criticism of Glasgow's transport system would, of course, be much more effective were the cutting remark to be made in the hearing of someone with some responsibility for the running of that system. It can, needless to add, be worked very effectively into a speech on any occasion when such an audience is within earshot.

The elderly Glasgow couple were in the process of migrating to Australia where they hoped to see their days out with their married daughter who had settled in a remote corner of that vast land. They were travelling by train to London, then from Tilbury to Sydney by ship, then by train and bus into the heart of the continent, and the final stages of their journey were to be made by ox wagon and other similar transport.

The journey, however, began in a Glasgow bus which took them from Dennistoun to Central Station, and it was as they stepped off the platform of this vehicle on to the comparative safety of the pavement in Union Street that the man was overheard to remark to his wife, 'Weel, Maggie, thank goodness that's the worst of the journey by.'

The number must be legion of the tales of clever quips by counsel, generally at the expense of the bench, but occasionally at that of the witnesses. An account of the famous trial of Oscar Wilde provides interesting material for any who would compile an anthology of such cross-cracks. I take my story, though, from those attributed to F E Smith.

After a particularly nasty exchange the judge remarked, I'm afraid, Mr Smith, we are both being very rude this morning. 'That is perfectly true, m'lud,' was the reply. 'The only difference between us is that I am doing it deliberately.'

There was a time, it is said, when in the Scottish courts braid Scots was used in pleadings, and this could lead to difficulties when, as in an appeal to the House of Lords from north of the border, there was a confrontation of the two tongues. In one such case it is recorded that the Scottish advocate began his pleading, 'I have here three pints, my Lord' only to be interrupted from the bench, 'But, Mr M'Adam, there are four of us!'

The one I like best, though, is the following.

The case had to do with the right of a proprietor to divert a stream and so deprive his neighbour of a supply of water. The whole gamut of decided cases in the matter of water rights was being rehearsed by a Scottish counsel in an English court, and in the best Scottish tradition he was rolling the word 'water' with a real splash to it. This was getting on the nerves of the judge who broke in at length – 'Tell me, Mr Andrew', he enquired, 'in that part of the world from which you come do they spell the word with two "t"s?' 'Naw, m'lord, but we spell the word "manners" wi' twa "n"s.'

For my own part though I find it hard to better the perfectly true tale of an exchange which took place in the Sheriff Court in Paisley a long number of years ago. Some part of my own appreciation of the exchange springs from my knowledge of the protagonists. It is so often the trouble that the funniest jokes are "in" affairs impossible to convey properly to the outsider.

Mr Alston Cameron, a solicitor from Johnstone, was waiting to go into the little Appeal Court at Paisley where the Sheriff Principal was shortly to be hearing appeals. Sheriff Hamilton, the Sheriff Substitute, came downstairs from his chambers on his way to his own court and had perforce to pass his ancient adversary on the way. 'Good morning, Mr Cameron,' he greeted him. 'You'll be hoping to have one of my decisions overturned this morning, I expect.'

'Oh no, your Lordship,' replied Mr Cameron, 'it's much worse than that – I'm hoping to have one of them upheld.'

Inevitably there is a rash of Winston Churchill stories that fall into this category. How many of these genuinely belong and how many are attributed I should not like to guess, for once a name becomes associated with a particular type of joke it is natural for cracks of that kind to be attributed to him. I content myself with quoting a couple at random.

It is said that Churchill was stopped one day in a corner of the House by Mr Anuerin Bevan who said, 'Winston, could you give me a couple of pennies – I want to phone one of my friends.'

Churchill handed him some coppers. 'Here's fourpence,' he said, 'Why don't you phone them both?'

Or again there was the time when Churchill was trying to dictate some correspondence to a typist in one of the little rooms available for interviewing and the like. He could not concentrate on what he was about for the noise of a voice booming away next door. Angrily he asked what was going on. 'That,' said the typist, 'is the honourable member for one of the Scottish constituencies talking to one of his people.' 'Why doesn't somebody tell him there's a telephone?' was the reply.

In the best Highland tradition it is possible for the barb to be introduced in so cannie and cautious a fashion as to delude the inexperienced into thinking it is the result of accident, not of design. This, even if it can be believed, makes it none the less painful. There was the Highland ghillie and the diluted whisky for example.

Donald, the ghillie, had spent the day rowing the American angler around the loch, without disturbing the resident fish overmuch. And now as the evening settled in they returned to the hotel where the visitor invited Donald to have a dram – an offer that was taken up with alacrity.

'Tell me, Mr Marshall,' said Donald after a preliminary sampling of his refreshment, 'which did you put in first, the wa-ater or the wheesky?'

'I put the Scotch in first and then I added the water – is that not the way you do it over here?'

'Ach now, that weel explain it all,' said Donald happy to have solved a mystery, 'the trouble ees that I will not haff got down to the wheesky yet.'

As is to be expected in Scotland the ministry comes in for its full share of this kind of nasty crack. Delivered with a perfectly straight face and with an air of the most profound solemnity this kind of attack is extraordinarily difficult to rebut. Indeed your best plan is to ignore it, pretending you haven't noticed the barb. Why give your tormentor the satisfaction of knowing he has hit home? And in any case what could you say by way of restoring your self-esteem if hit square-on as happened to this poor chap?

> The minister was expounding a principle which, he claimed he invariably followed – to wit, that at any time when he had to be away from home it was his unfailing custom to ensure that his pulpit was filled by someone who was a better preacher than he was.
>
> Remarked one of his hearers, 'Man I'm thinkin' yer choice will no' be sair restricted.'

Or how do you respond to the lady who gets you in the solar plexus like this – assuming, that is, that she leaves you with enough breath to be able to reply!

> The preacher was standing in the kirk doorway bidding adieu to the departing congregation and accepting with due modesty congratulatory remarks about his sermon from this one and from that. So that when one lady, shaking him warmly by the hand, enquired, 'Mr Brown, did anyone ever tell you that you're just wonderful?' he was not taken wholly by surprise. He hastened, however, to explain that no-one had ever put it in these precise words. In which case came the riposte, 'Then where in all the world did you get the idea that you are?'

Sometimes, of course, it is possible and even tempting to assume that the offending remark was not intended to be offensive but represented merely an observation that might have been more tactfully phrased. Such might well be the case in the following instance, though from what I know of country humour I would take a good deal of convincing that the point was not both clearly seen and deliberately planned. The prime purpose might well be to be funny, but the fact that the joke had a cutting edge to it would be a not unwelcome bonus.

> The minister's car had broken down and he had got a tow to a nearby country garage. After due inspection the mechanic gave it as his opinion that something quite radical was at fault, requiring a quite considerable job in both time and materials. 'Well,' said the minister resignedly, 'if that's the way things are there's nothing for it but just to go ahead. But try to be as quick as possible, for I need the car very badly. And go as easy as you can on the bill, for I'm just a poor preacher.'

'I ken,' said the garage proprietor, 'I heard you in oor kirk the ither Sunday.'

But I'm sure that the beadle in the following tale was merely following his normal philosophical bent and had no intention of being offensive.

The young preacher had headed for the pulpit full of zip and confidence, but had made rather a mess of the service, so that he returned to the vestry sadly crestfallen in spirit.

'Man' said the beadle (a philosopher in private life) 'it's juist like this, if ye had gaed up thae poopit stairs the way ye cam' doon, ye might hae cam' doom the way ye gaed up.'

I wouldn't be prepared, though, to vouch for the *bona fide*s of the beadle in this other case. I happen to know him.

The minister, from the very start, had been making heavy weather of an old sermon, but he got really deep into the mire when he turned over to the last page to find that it wasn't there. He managed to finish somehow, and afterwards in the vestry he was telling the beadle of his plight. He just couldn't imagine what had happened to the missing page. Anxious as always to be helpful the beadle came up with the bright suggestion, 'Maybe the moths have got at it.'

Not all such cracks are directed first hand at the person criticised. There's a very nice little yarn about the man who had obviously been much wearied by over-long discourses.

The small boy was attending Church for the first time and was anxious to understand what it was all about. When the organist came in, took his seat at the consol, set up his music, pulled out a few stops, and so on the wee fellow enquired excitedly, 'Daddy, what does that mean?' An explanation was hurriedly whispered. Again when the beadle solemnly carried in The Book the question was put, 'Daddy, what does that mean?' Again a whispered explanation. And so on right through the service till they came to the sermon. At this point the minister ostentatiously unstrapped the watch from his wrist and placed it on the bookboard. 'Daddy what does that mean?' With a bitterness born of long experience, Father replied, 'Believe me, Sonny, it doesn't mean a single thing.'

Talking of the small boy attending Church for the first time tempts me to digress and tell of the little chap who had been taken by his father to his first service, and that in an old-fashioned building with box pews with doors to them, fitted with the narrowest of seats, so high that only the tallest could sit with their feet resting on the ground, and with backs so angled as to prevent the dullest sermon from putting anyone to sleep. Asked afterwards about his experience the youthful martyr explained, 'My faither opened a press door an' we a' sat on a shelf.'

Out of the mouths of babes and sucklings, indeed.

And then there's the tale of the woman whose distaste of read sermons was equalled only by her horror of having the singing led by instrumental music.

The newly inducted minister of a country parish read not only his sermon but his prayers as well. He was, however, of a musical bent and raised money for the purchase of a grand harmonium to take the place of the aged precentor who had been accustomed to 'give the note' for the singing on a Sunday.

Two members of the congregation met in the street and the one remarked that it was a long time since she had seen her friend in the kirk – had she been ill. 'No, an' ye'll no' be seein' me there for a while.'

'Why, what's the matter. It's not like you to miss being at the kirk.'

'There's plenty the matter. As if it wasna bad enough to have a paper minister, noo we've gotten a wooden precentor.'

To conclude this group of tales of an ecclesiastical character here is a story which has a distinctly ecumenical flavour, if the predominating ingredient is acid.

A dyed-in-the-vestments Anglican high-churchman was describing his attitude towards the non-conformists, of whom it seemed there was an unconscionably large number in his parish. His reaction could briefly be described as less than sympathetic.

'Would you baptise their children?' he was asked.

'Most emphatically not.'

'Would you unite a pair of them in the bonds of holy matrimony?' the questioner persisted.

'They could cohabit in sin till kingdom come before I would marry them.'

'Surely at least you would bury one of them?'

Without hesitation came the reply, 'With the greatest satisfaction in the world I would bury the lot of them.'

Can you imagine anything better calculated to put a speaker off his balance than an interchange like the following – can you think up a suitable, let alone a suitably cutting, reply? And yet there's nothing strictly defamatory about the wisecrack, it's just a plain unvarnished statement of fact. To make matters worse it was the speaker himself who triggered it all off in the first place.

The speaker was conscious of having lost the attention of a man sitting at the back of the hall. This he felt must be due to faulty acoustics – the material was interesting enough. Pausing, therefore, in his address he solicitously enquired, 'I wonder if I'm being heard all right by the gentleman at the back?'

'I'm hearing you perfectly,' said the occupant of the back seat. And then he added, 'but I'd be more than happy to swop seats with anyone who isn't.'

The element of fun exceeds the element of acid in the following inerchange on the football field – although in the ordinary run of things referees are liable to come in for more acid than fun. Like the man in black who said to the angry player, 'The very last thing I want is any unpleasantness.' 'Have you any other last requests?' was the unsympathetic rejoinder.

It was at once cruel and foul the way the inside forward had been tackled – and that inside the penalty box. Turning a blind eye, however, to the man writhing on the ground, the referee waved on play. Realising how ineffective was his dumb show of agony the player arose and turned his attention to providing in a loud voice a thumb-nail character sketch of the man with the whistle.

This at least was productive of results. The referee stopped play and, producing his wee black book and pencil, he beckoned the offender towards him. 'Will you, he said, be so good as to repeat what you've just been saying.'

'Goad,' said the exasperated player, 'you don't mean to tell me that you're deaf as well as blind.'

While there's humour enough there's little kindliness in either of the following pair of true stories from the country.

'My word is as good as my bond,' pompously proclaimed the First Party to the proposed contract to which he was most reluctant to sign.

'In spite of that warning,' responded the Second Party magnanimously, 'I shall still be prepared to accept your bond. So will you please sign on the dotted line.'

Or what about this one.

The manager's minion approached the works engineer, 'The manager wants to know, Willie, what's he to do with that old transformer that's taking up room in the garage. He says I've to ask you, will he hang on to it or will he just throw it in the river?'

'Tell him,' replied the engineer, 'juist to throw it in the river.' And then the cruel postscript – 'And tell him to hang on to it at the same time.'

Again from the country comes this one.

The back seat of the car was packed with trophies of their Sunday afternoon in the country – branches of trees, armfuls of wild flowers, cuttings of this and that – the lot. Unfortunately, however, in their zeal for collecting specimens they had lost their way.

Spotting a local resident at the roadside they pulled up, and the driver, leaning out of the window of his laden vehicle, enquired graciously, 'Tell me, my good man, can I take this road back to the city?'

'I suppose you might as well,' replied the local yokel, 'you seem to be taking damn near everything else.'

Farmers are notoriously cautious. It could be said of them that they would never dream of counting their chickens after they are hatched – they would rather wait until they started laying. And when it comes to parting with siller their native quality of caution can really assert itself.

In the old days before the tractor when every factor had its quota of pairs-of-horses it was a regular thing during May and June to pass on the road a man leading a stallion. The financial background to the services of this itinerant sire was that a down-payment was made at the beginning of the season for every mare that was to be served, and then if and when she had a foal a further payment fell due. This second instalment was called 'foal-money' and it was customary for the man who had trudged the country with the stallion to take the road again collecting the said foal-money.

It was said of one such traveller that when asked if he was getting his money in all right he replied ruefully, 'I think some of them are waiting to see what kind of workers they turn out before they part wi' the siller.'

Judges at cattle-shows fall into a category very similar to that of referees at football matches – incompetence and corruption are among the kindlier of the charges laid against them. I met a farmer one day who I knew had been parading a Clydesdale filly at Ayr show a few days earlier and had taken third prize. Feigning ignorance I enquired how it had gone with the filly at Ayr. 'They judged her first,' he replied without hesitation. 'Oh,' I said, rather taken aback in view of my very different information, 'I'm very glad to hear that.' 'Ay,' he said, 'ye see they handed oot the first two tickets to their freends, and then they started to judge them.'

Farmers can also be 'real mean' in the American sense of that expression – that is to say in their tendency to let you have the whole truth without much consideration for your feelings. This from the butcher's shop.

The farmer had been complaining about the quality of last week's joint which, he claimed, had been tough beyond description. 'I had to file my teeth to get through it.'

'The trouble with the beef today,' the butcher explained, 'is that it's not killed long enough.'

'The trouble wi' that roast ye sold me,' rejoined the farmer, 'was that it wasna killed soon enough.'

Which leads me to move the scene to a city restaurant for the following exchanges.

'How did you find your steak, sir?' solicitously enquired the waiter as he took away the empty plate.

'Quite by accident,' replied the less-than-satisfied diner, 'it was concealed behind the potato.'

If it wasn't the same diner it must have been the same restaurant that was involved in this exchange.

'What's this?' as a plate of muddy fluid was laid before him.

'That's bean soup, sir.'

'I'm not the least interested in its history – what I want to know is what it is now.'

But as usual it takes a lady to have the last word.

As a highly indignant customer clamoured, 'Miss, there's a fly in my soup,' the lady retorted, 'wheest, don't speak so loud, dearie, they'll all be wantin' wan.'

Mothers-in-law down through the centuries have had a way of finding themselves at the receiving end of the dirty crack. I take it everyone knows the definition of 'mixed feelings' as the emotional reaction of a man on learning that his mother-in-law has just reversed his split-new Jaguar over the cliff. And the following is surely no more kindly, even if it is a shade more stupid.

The man had arrived at the vet's surgery with a dog that was clearly of high pedigree. He wanted its tail docked – right back to the rump. The vet protested. A bushy tail was a feature of this particular breed, he had rarely seen a finer example of such a tail than that attached to the dog before him, to interfere with it would be utter folly – and more in the same strain.

The man was adamant – the tail had to go.

'But tell me, why are you so determined to have the beast docked?'

'Well it's like this. Next Monday the wife's mother's comin' to stay with us for a month and I don't want there to be one single sign of welcome.'

To take a kindlier note I turn to the following anecdote from the realm of connubial bliss.

They had decided to mark the fiftieth anniversary of their

wedding, had John and Janet, by treating themselves to a West Highland holiday. John had gone to considerable pains to plan this, and he had included a couple of days on the Island of Skye, which they were to leave by ferry on the second evening to take up a booking on the mainland, with the result that they found themselves running for the last ferry that would take them across to the mainland and the room and the meal that awaited them there. Unhappily Janet lacked the necessary turn of speed and the boat departed without them.

A good deal of trailing hither and yonder and they at length secured a somewhat indifferent room and an unimaginative meal – and John was not at his happiest or most jovial. Later as they were preparing for bed Janet was brushing her luxuriant grey hair. 'Ay, John,' she said, 'I've maybe got winter in my hair, but I've still got summer in my heart.'

The only response was a grunt and the observation, 'If ye had had a wee thing mair spring in yer heel we never had missed that boat.'

It is perhaps fitting, though, that this section should turn for its last word to the Scriptures.

The minister generally felt much encouraged when people turned up in their own Bibles the text of his sermon. He felt this manifested an anticipatory interest in what he was about to say. He made an exception, however, in the case of Thomas, an old member and a most regular attender who sat in the front pew, for Thomas not only turned up the text, but having found it he produced a pencil with which he wrote the day's date in the margin. This to the preacher seemed to be taking a quite unfair advantage.

One week, having been hard pressed with pastoral duties, the minister decided to preach an old sermon, but, having Thomas in mind, he found a text quite suitable to the content of the sermon though in a different part of the Book from the one used on the earlier occasion.

Out of the corner of his eye he watched with interest as Thomas turned up the place and made his annotation in the virgin white of the margin. Meeting Thomas after the service and well pleased with himself for his successful deception, the minister enquired,

'Well, Thomas, and what did you think of the sermon this morning?'

'Oh aye, verra guid, aye verra guid, I liked it fine. But dae ye ken what I'm gonna tell ye, minister, I think I liked it fully better last time to its richt text.'

It rather reminds me of an old friend who used to say that he hated preaching an old sermon, for he found himself concluding either that they remembered it and were despising him for the repetition, or that they didn't remember a single thing about it, in which case he was despising himself for preaching such unmemorable rubbish.

You just can't win.

CHAPTER NINE

THE SCHOOLBOY HOWLER

OVER THE CENTURIES THE CLASSROOM has been a most fruitful garden of merriment. The jokes have ranged from the simple mistake arising from honest ignorance (the boy who wrote that his hero mounted his hors de combat and rode from the field), through the plain mis-spelling (the boy in the Bible exam who claimed that in our Lord's time they had no proper carpets and so had to make do with rough mating on the floor), and the use of the synonym which unhappily is not synonymous (the lad who discovered the gas escaping fluently through a burst pipe), to the much more highly sophisticated lady who was painfully fussy about correct pronunciation so that when her young nephew drew attention to 'that dug' she said, 'Surely Willam, it's not a dug.' 'Weel auntie it's awfu' like a dug.'

It is a realm where there can be considerable temptation to invent, and it has often seemed to me that some highly sophisticated howlers owe a good deal to the imagination. I refer to efforts such as that about the class who were to bring an object representative of the Bible and someone brought a deceased bee which he declared represented 'Nahum'; for the question there is even more stupid than the answer. Or the little girl who wanted to call her teddy 'Gladly' because the hymn said 'Gladly my cross-eye'd bear'. It's not a pinch but a cellar-full of salt that's needed to make these tick. Or even the one about the boy who when asked to write a sentence containing the word 'sojourn' produced, 'My father was a sojourn in the war.' Stories of that calibre have always appealed to me as an insult to youthful ignorance.

To me, incidentally, it occurs that to talk about the schoolboy howler may itself be something of a howler. Perhaps we should rename it the school-young-person howler. It is just possible on the other hand that this is a realm where the ladies do not want to compete, that the feminists are content to leave the male sex with a monopoly of the stupidity represented by the howler. To be on the safe side I'll take pains to ensure that in any case where I quote a boy as the near-idiot of the tale the hero couldn't possibly have been a heroine. Greatly daring I might suggest in passing that some of the efforts to avoid a male connotation in the use of terms can lead to results almost on a par with the schoolboy howler. 'Chairperson' I regard as bad enough. I am awaiting with interest that when a girl graduates in theology she should be capped 'Spinster of Theology.'

You never know what kids pick up – sometimes as a result of our careless pronunciation – as in the case of the child who thought the Lord's Prayer went 'Harold be thy name'; or the other who defined the equator as 'a menagerie lion running round the centre of the world.' I remember a Bible exam in which a youthful member of the Boys' Brigade wrote that our Lord called Matthew to be his disciple from 'the reset of costumes.' Not so bad, perhaps, as the following.

> The teacher had explained that the 'taxing' referred to in the Christmas story as having been first made when Cyrenius was governor of Syria and which was responsible for our Lord being born in Bethlehem, was a kind of census. It was understandable, therefore, that when one of the class was asked why Joseph and Mary had gone to Bethlehem she answered without hesitation that they had gone there 'in order to be censured.'

It was a school-teacher in my first parish who told of this howler perpetrated in his own school. They had had a lesson about volcanoes in general and about Vesuvius in particular. They were to follow this up by writing a composition under the title, 'My Visit to Vesuvius'. One child having described how they set out before dawn went on to the remarkable disclosure, 'Just as dawn broke we looked up and there was the Creator smoking at the top of the hill.' It was after the same lesson on volcanoes that yet another child defined a crater as a 'poor old soul.' A Bible lesson about the woman at the well elicited at question time the surprising information that a pitcher is 'a thing with wood all round it that you hang on the wall'. Then there was the boy who said that in some countries a man is allowed to have as many wives as he likes and this is called polygamy, but in this country it is illegal to have more than one wife and this is called monotony.

Perhaps this true yarn from the Galloway country should more properly find a place in the chapter dealing with jokes that are 'near the bone', but I think the fact that it is so free of malice aforethought justifies its inclusion here. The five-year-old had arrived at school for his first day. After being encouraged to sit around for a time and look at a book of pictures he was given a couple of sweeties and put out to play for ten minutes. On his return he was issued with some Plasticine and told to get on with a bit of modelling. A glass of milk and another short interval in the playground ensued. Then he was told to form a circle on the floor with some other kids and they were given blocks and toys with which to entertain themselves. The day was now far advanced and shortly afterwards the little chap was sent home. The second day looked like being a repetition of the first. But Gavin was for none of it. Leaving his Plasticine he came over to the teacher. 'Miss,' he said, 'I thought I had come here for tae learn for tae coont.' The title here must surely be 'Life is real, life is earnest,' as of course it was for those wresting a living out of some of those southern hills.

There are times of course when the schoolboy howler is in effect a criticism of the teaching. For it reveals how the little mind has been working and how it has been put off the rails simply because the teacher wasn't sufficiently imaginative – or maybe sufficiently awake – to foresee and guard against the chances of misunderstanding.

I remember a country minister telling me in tones of bitterness and scorn just what a bunch of mental defectives he had in his Bible Class. He had been trying to inculcate some understanding of the doctrine of the Holy Spirit (an ambitious task I thought if they were all that dumb) and had seemingly made a great deal of the idea of incorporeality. They had obviously been listening even if they had been construing things differently from what was intended, for one youth on being asked to explain his conception of the Holy Spirit instantly replied, 'All head and legs – no body.' It is a pity, certainly, when a disembodied spirit comes to be visualised as a kind of human tadpole, but you can see how the idea got abroad.

As I have said, we do not always try hard enough to understand how young minds are working, nor do we always allow for the number of terms that are commonplace to us but incomprehensible to them. For instance, they may not know about temples, but supermarkets are a matter of everyday experience. And for those readers who are not acquainted with the West of Scotland it has to be explained that 'Templetons' is the name of a chain of supermarkets in these parts with, obviously, a branch in the town to which this little chap would be taken by his parents on their shopping outing on a Saturday afternoon. Hence his mental picture, vivid enough even if, through no fault of his, not quite accurate. The teacher had been telling her little charges the story of the visit of the young Jesus with his parents to Jerusalem and of how he came to be left there and was later found talking with the doctors in the temple. Going over the story later with one small boy she elicited the tale of the missing child and of how the anxious parents retraced their steps towards the city with heavy hearts. 'Oh but they found him a' richt when they got back to the toon,' the little fellow reassured her. 'And where was it that they found him?' she enquired. 'He was talkin' to some men in Templeton's.'

Before the onset of the tractor each farm had its quota of horses and carts, and in many cases the latter included a special type of vehicle called a 'Jenny Lind'. I don't know the origin of the name, but the cart was a flat affair with extensions over the wheels designed for the bringing in of the sheaves at harvest. Where the shafts and body met, was a plate bearing – sometimes in brass, often in blue enamel – the name of the owner and of his farm. It is essential today to fill in this background material for the comprehension of this story from a country Sunday School. It illustrates again how the child can be building up the story in clear and specific mental pictures.

Laboriously the teacher had taken them on the trail of Joseph from the day his brothers sold him into slavery in Egypt, through his foretelling of the seven years when the crops would fail following the years of plenty, to his exalted position in charge of the national grain reserves during the days of the famine. Readers of Genesis will remember that when Joseph's brothers came down to Egypt in search of corn although he instantly recognised them they had no clue as to his identity. The teacher wondered whether anyone could tell her why this should have been so. 'He was an awful lot older,' came one answer, 'Yes, but they were older too, why should Joseph have known them right away?' There was a moment or two's silence until one little chap piped up, 'He would see their name om the cairts.'

There, you see, was someone who had been picturing the whole thing vividly in terms of his own situation. If you pause for a moment it does conjure up a wonderful picture of a fleet of Jenny Linds each bearing its name-plate 'Jacob & Sons, Schemen Mains'. Well, dash it all, they had come to buy corn, and they had to have some conveyance to take it home. Today I expect he would have said he recognised their tractor!

The child is nothing if not a literalist. Once he has learnt an answer he can be counted on to give it, and to feel sore cheated if it turns out to be for any reason, other than correct. Like the not-very-bright pupil who was asked 'Nine times seven' and after quite a bit of cogitation came up with the answer 'Sixty-three.' 'Quite good,' said the teacher. 'Quite good my bunnet,' said the boy, 'it's bloomin perfect.' To return, however to our literalist.

The aged parish minister had faithfully visited his one-teacher school year after year for as long as memory stretched to examine the children in their saving knowledge of the things of God. Invariably he asked the same questions in the identical order and always he gave timeous warning of his impending visit. The obvious method of coping with a situation like this was to have each child coached in the correct answer to the specific question he was going to be asked. Why try to impart a vague smear of knowledge over a whole field when you can lay it on concentrated over the only part of the field that matters? The catechism began, 'Who made you?' then 'What were you made of?' next, 'Where did you first live?' and, 'What were the names of the first couple?' and so on. The system had worked perfectly for years until one day the old chap arrived and was welcomed as usual. He delivered his standard introductory remarks leading up to 'just one or two simple questions . . . You, the first boy in the back seat, who made you?'

'Please sir, "dust",' came the unhesitating reply.

'Come now, think what you are saying, my boy. Who made you?'

With an even greater air of confidence came the assurance that it was dust that had made him.

'But surely, sonny, it was God who made you.'

'No, sir, the boy that God made is in bed with the cold.'

An old minister neighbour of my own who was a regular visitor at the village school used to take great delight in asking the class, 'If there were three crows perched on a gate and I came along and shot the middle one how many crows would there still be on the gate?' Invariably this was treated as a problem in simple arithmetic and he got the obvious answer reached by subtraction. He laughed at this, for he felt that as country children they ought to have been sufficiently alert to make allowance for the habits of winged creatures when guns are going off around them. For myself I had a lot of sympathy with these children. All arithmetical problems are based upon the assumption that outside factors are irrelevant and may therefore be ignored – that, in fact, other things are equal. (May I pause to interject that it is alarming how many people insist on saying 'all things being equal.' It'll be a dull world indeed when that state of affairs is achieved.) Take the business of ratios. If three men build a wall in four days how many days will it take for six men to do the job? Now every schoolboy knows the answer is two days. Yet I might quite well give you the answer 'ten days.' And when asked to explain how that could be say that the shop-steward had just been along to tell the men there was a go-slow in operation. And the habits of shop-stewards are every bit as unpredictable as those of crows.

One of the troubles, as I have said, is that once he has got hold of something it can be mighty hard to persuade him that he ought to let go. The young schoolboy refused to be convinced that the past participle of the verb 'to write' is 'written' – in his book it was 'wrote'. With a view to impressing the correct form indelibly on his memory the teacher instructed him to write out 'I have written' five hundred times. When at length his task was accomplished four o'clock was passed and the boy could find no-one with whom to entrust the evidence of his diligence. So he left the sheets on the teacher's desk along with a note which read, 'I have wrote I have written five hundred times and have now went home.'

The following is not really a howler but rather a nice example of the innocent way in which the young person can get away with a crack that might get his elders into trouble.

> The new boy had just disembarked at the school gate from a magnificent chauffeur-driven, highly polished limousine. 'Jings that's a braw car o' yer faither's,' commented his pal. 'Ay' said the new arrival. Then he added casually, 'We've another three at home exactly the same – forby the hearse.'

In many of these stories the point of the joke lies in the fact that while the children are using the same language as their elders they are working from a different scale of values, and it is the confrontation of these contradictions that produces the laugh. Take a simple example. If on a train journey someone asks anxiously about a town on the route it will not surprisingly be assumed that he wants to get off there, but, particularly with a young person, that may be quite a wrong conclusion.

> As the little chap boarded the Stranraer train in Glasgow he said to the guard, 'My mummy said I was to be sure to ask you to tell me when we got to Ayr.' The man in uniform undertook that he would be timeously informed. A quarter of an hour after leaving Glasgow the train pulled up at Paisley and the boy was anxiously hanging out of the carriage window demanding to know if this was Ayr. 'We've still a long way to go to Ayr, sonny. Just you sit down and content yourself and I'll tell you when we get there.' This, however, did little to reassure the child, and every time the train

stopped he was convinced they must now be at Ayr. When at length they did reach Ayr the guard, mindful of his promise, hurried along to where the boy was, opened the compartment door, 'Right, son, out you get, this is Ayr.' 'Oh but I'm not getting out here,' explained the child, 'I'm going on to my grannie's at Stranraer. But my mummy said I could could eat my piece when we got to Ayr.'

Mark you, that kind of thing is not necessarily confined to children. There comes to mind a different version of what is essentially the same story, at least with the identical clash of conclusions.

A charming young member of the Wrens, heavily encumbered with luggage, boarded the crowded Gouock train. A corner seat was gladly surrendered by one gallant youth who explained that he preferred standing. Other chivalrous young fellows competed for the privilege of putting the various items of luggage on the rack. The train in due course pulled up at Bishopton, and after a moment or two the young lady enquired, 'Is this Bishopton?' About half-a-dozen young men simultaneously replied in the affirmative and hustled to get the door opened and her various packages out on to the platform. 'It's Port Glasgow I'm going to,' she added in the most disarming tones. 'But you see my friend told me it was the second stop after Bishopton.'

We are assured that children today mature more quickly than was the case a century ago. This for my own part I would beg leave to doubt. What I would not challenge for a moment is that children today display a degree of self-confidence and acquire a veneer of sophistication utterly unknown in the days of good Queen Vic, as is highlighted in this tale.

The parents of the twelve-year old boy were a bit worried as they saw him off alone on a fairly long plane journey. They had taken the precaution, however, of asking the airline people to pay particular attention to him. The plane had not been airborne more than a few minutes, seat-belts were being unfastened, cigarettes were being lit, when a ravishing hostess (aren't they all?) appeared at the boy's side, explained to him that he need have no worries, that she personally would be looking after him, and ended up wondering whether there was anything she could get him right now. 'Thanks,' he said, 'I would like a brandy and soda.' Looking at him in quizzical fashion she remarked, 'What you want is to get me into trouble.' 'Yes,' he replied, 'that's right. But all in its own good time. At the present moment all I'm askin for is a brandy and soda.'

I was talking earlier about the inability of the child to rest content so long as there is 'a piece' uneaten, and that is reminiscent of what is not a schoolboy howler but an example of schoolboy impudence.

The policemen had caught two small boys red-handed in the perpetration of some mischief. The matter was not of sufficient gravity to be the subject of formal report and follow-up, but was much too serious to be completely ignored. It was clearly a case for instilling some fear of the law – if not of the Lord – into the young minds. And the day when this could be achieved by a 'buff on the lug' was past. So after a threatening talking-to the officers left the two boys locked in the police-box ostensibly to await the arrival of the black maria that would convey them to the cells for a spell on bread and water. Having left them thus to their own devices for an hour and more the bobbies returned, and after a further dressing-down they released their prisoners. The kids took to their heels – as far as the next street-corner. There they stopped to make various jeering noises in the direction of the officers. Not that the latter were unduly upset at that. But they were quite a bit disturbed when the unrepentent ones began to shout, 'We werena frichted at a'; an' we fairly enjoyed your sandwiches.'

There are parts of the country – and even more particularly of the city – where relations between children and the forces of law and order are not of the best.

In an attempt to improve relations between police and people in one of the city's worst areas of deprivation it was thought wise for an officer to visit the local school and talk to the kids in the friendliest way, for this was essentially a public relations exercise. His talk, suitably illustrated with clips of film, entertaining little stories and exciting exhibits on how the public can co-operate with the force elicited a great deal of interest, and the teacher followed it up, setting an essay on 'The Police'. One small boy not greatly skilled in literary pursuits produced a single – but telling – sentence, 'The polis is devils.' The teacher was not a little amused and took an early opportunity to inform the policeman that he had failed to win an ally in the case of at least one of his audience. 'Ah, just give me time,' said the officer, noting the identity of the writer. Next evening as the school was skailing a police Jaguar drew in at the kerb and Master Mischief was invited to come for a ride. In due course they returned to headquarters where a visit was paid to the canteen for fish and chips. A pleasant time was then had in the gym. In due course he was driven home in the Jag to come again some other day. A fresh essay was called for to allow the wee fellow to put into words his fresh assessment of the force. Again a single sentence – but this time it read, 'The polis is cunning devils.'

As I have remarked earlier, children's values do not always match up with ours, the disparity leading to amusing situations as in this exchange, overheard in my own country parish.

The pair of ten-year-olds, William and Robert, were the closest of friends though they came from social backgrounds that were poles apart. William was the only child of a widowed mother and his upbringing included the entire cotton-wool treatment. Bobbie, on the other hand, was one of a family of ten where both parents went out to work and, in the country phrase, he had been allowed to hang as he grew. The two boys were playing one afternoon in William's garden when mama appeared at the window. 'Come away in, William, and get washed,' she said, 'it's nearly tea-time.' Bobbie whose cleanliness was of concern to none was understandably sympathetic. 'Ach, Willie,' he said, 'it's a dirty shame; they're forever washin' at ye.'

Among adults themselves, of course, there can be a considerable difference of standards, so that a situation like the following can easily arise.

A small boy with a lollipop had boarded a busy bus with his mother and had got down to share a seat with a lady in a magnificent new mink coat. The unhappy wearer was undergoing agonies of apprehension as the wet lolly was waved around, missing her pride and joy by miraculous millimetres. Great, naturally, was her relief when from a couple of seats back came the warning, 'Tommie, son, watch what ye're daein' wavin' that lolly o' yours aboot near that woman's fur coat. If you're no' careful you'll get it covered in hair.'

That story was brought vividly to my mind one day as I was going along a Glasgow side street full of parked cars. A small boy was standing on the bonnet of one of them and had just finished submitting the bonnet-lid to the trampoline test. He was now busily engaged drawing his sticky fingers along the windscreen. Two women stood talking on the edge of the pavement. One of them turned round and seeing what her son was up to commanded, 'Come doon aff that car, Reginald, you'll get yersel' a' dirty afore ever we start.'

The loyalty of a child can produce quite entertaining results as evidenced in this interchange.

> Three schoolboys were discussing the respective earning-power of their parents. The first explained that his father was a surgeon and was liable to collect a fee of anything upwards of £100 for the simplest operation. The second one capped this by claiming that his dad, who was a concert violinist, would not dream of walking on to a concert platform for a consideration of anything less than £500. The third boy, a son of the manse, might have been thought to be at something of a disadvantage playing in this league. Not a bit of it. He proudly proclaimed, 'That's nothing. When my daddy preaches a sermon on a Sunday morning it takes six men to carry down the collection.'

I think this well-known tale should properly be regarded as a parental rather than a schoolboy howler.

> The proud mother had foregathered with the teacher on the street and was taking the opportunity to enquire what progress her young hopeful was making. 'He's quite a clever boy,' said the teacher, 'in fact his biggest trouble is that he can sometimes be a wee bit too smart. I'll give you an instance. One day last week we were doing history and I said to him, 'Who signed Magna Carta?' And he said, 'Please miss, it wasna' me.'
>
> 'The little ne-er do well,' said his mother. 'Wait till I get my hands on him. It would be him all the time.'

Upon this simple foundation there has been built, in a shaggy dog kind of fashion, a most elaborate and complicated tale.

The school chaplain had been giving instruction to one of the classes for an hour and on handing them back to their regular teacher he reported – for the latter's enjoyment – that one of the boys on being asked who had pulled down the walls of Jericho had replied, 'Sir, it wasn't me.' So far from being amused the teacher was much concerned. 'What boy did you say that was?' The chaplain mentioned a name. 'Well,' said the teacher, 'all I can say is that that lad is one of the most trustworthy characters I have ever come across. If he says he didn't do it then I'm sure you must look for the culprit elsewhere.' The chaplain did not pursue the subject further – how can you in a case like that? But such was his amusement that he sought out the headmaster and passed the whole yarn on to him. 'But this is a most unfortunate affair,' opined that gentleman in the most solemn tones. 'You see, Mr Bradley is one of my very best teachers, and I would hate to think of any kind of official investigation being set on foot that seemed to cast doubts on his disciplinary methods.'

By this time amusement had given place to incredulity. So much so that the chaplain went straight to the Education Offices where he sought out the Director who, he felt sure, would share his horror at this massive ignorance of Scripture. Instead however, the Director, having heard the whole story said, 'This looks like the beginning of a very awkward situation. I hate to think what this could lead to if once the press got hold of it. I tell you what – by far the simplest plan if you are agreeable – is for us to arrange quietly with the Master of Works to have that bit of wall rebuilt and we'll just put it through the report as storm damage.'

This next one is not in any sense a schoolboy howler, but it's a most lovely little tale that illustrates vividly the distinctive position accorded to the minister in the Scottish village of a century ago.

The old lady was walking along the village street with her young grandson held firmly by the hand. All of a sudden his arm suffered a violent jerk.

'Strachten your bunnet, Willie,' she commanded, 'here's the minister's dug.'

There come to my mind a couple of tales that by no stretch of the imagination could be called schoolboy howlers – a more likely title would be Schoolboy Horrors.

As the result of an odd set of circumstances my wife and I some years ago found ourselves, more or less accidentally, spending a few days' holiday in a guest-house in the Yorkshire Dales. In the same house, also more or less accidentally, Freddie Grisewood of BBC fame and his wife were spending a few days. The four of us had the house to ourselves, and, believe me, we had some cheery evenings. Freddy's knowledge of the early days of broadcasting was quite unrivalled, so he had plenty of tales to tell, and he had great gifts as a raconteur – and what a voice! Here was one of his yarns – nothing to do with the BBC – but good hearing before a blazing fire on an autumn evening.

> The film was a much publicised spectacular of the Ben Hur period and style. When the story reached that point where the poor defenceless Christians were being thrown to the ravenous lions – all in glorious technicolour – a small boy in the audience began to weep loudly and copiously. His mother sought to comfort him with the assurance that no real harm was coming to the good people – it was only a picture. Her son, however, assured her that it was not for the Christians he was shedding tears but for 'that poor wee lion in the corner that doesn't have a Christian.'

My own contribution by way of retaliation for this was the following.

> Going along the street one morning a lady came upon a small boy standing disconsolate at the pavement weeping his heart out. 'What is it sonny? Whatever's the matter?' she enquired. Through the sobbing she was just able to make out, 'My faither's drooned the pups.'
> That, she agreed was a really heart-breaking thing to have happened, but, after all, it was one of the grim facts of life. Maybe, she ventured, his dog would have pups some other time and he would be allowed to keep one of them.
> 'But,' howled the disconsolate youth, 'it was me that was to get droonin' the pups.'

Closely akin to the schoolboy story so far as the element of humour is concerned is the story about the person with learning difficulties. It is a deep-set characteristic of human nature to laugh at the unusual, so I suppose it is natural that our first reaction is a smile when we hear or see something utterly different from what we had expected. That anyone should want to do things dramatically differently from us appears laughable. The funny-peculiar is not really so far removed from the funny-ha-ha. I imagine, therefore, it's the failure of the disturbed mind to produce normal reactions that leads to the smile.

Let me begin, however, with a little tale that comes from the region between honest simplicity and the stupidity that verges on genius, or at least, that demands a fair degree of ability.

A motorist driving in a remote corner of the north of Scotland had arrived at a point where he was confronted by a railway level crossing. But it was different from any he had ever seen before in that the gates seemed to be set in a kind of half-way position suitable for neither car nor train. The motorist was unwilling to take risks. Seeing a man in uniform he approached him and said, 'What does this mean? Your gates are half-shut.' 'Well, you see,' said Hamish, 'I am kind of half expecting a train.'

That mildly amusing one, however, becomes really funny when the slow learner has the last word.

The honorary degree of Doctor of Divinity had been conferred on The Rev William Worthy, minister of a country parish, to the great delight and satisfaction of his parishioners and of the family at the manse in particular. Some weeks after the graduation the minister's wife was walking down the village street when she was joined by Davie the village simpleton. As usual he was full of chatter. 'And how is Mr Worthy keeping?' he enquired. 'Davie,' the Lady of the Manse replied, 'everybody now calls my husband "Doctor Worthy".'

'Dae ye tell me that?' responded David. 'It's a terrible place this for geein' folk names. D'ye ken this, they ca me Garibaldi.'

Or perhaps the effect is even more shattering in this 'Guessing Game.'

It was obvious that the party in the car had lost their way amid the network of narrow roads. For while there was no want of cross-roads there was a great dearth of sign-posts. At length as they were approaching yet another crossing the driver was happy to see a young lad standing just where a sign-post should have been. Drawing alongside he enquired, 'Tell me, Jimmie, which is the road to Auchterloonie?' 'How did ye ken my name was Jimmie?' countered the youth. 'I just guessed,' humoured the driver. 'Well, if you're a' that guid at guessin' wad ye no' be better juist to guess the road to Auchterloonie!'

Another example of the soft answer that turneth away wrath?

An alarmingly large number of girls visiting the Manse to seek baptism for their fatherless bairns had named William M'Merry, a farm worker in a neighbouring parish, as the guilty party. The minister decided that the said William was much in need of a talking-to, so he sought him out and to his amazement found him to be a miserably plain, uncouth, unattractive character lacking in any of the graces and charms he had thought would have been essential for the winning of so many hearts. Having read Bill a homily on the need to mend his ways the minister concluded, 'Frankly, the one thing I cannot understand is how you manage to get round all these girls.' 'There's nae trouble aboot that,' said William, anxious to dispel the mystery, 'I've got a bike.'

The best of them all is this tale with its nice distinction between slow learning and stupidity.

It was just outside the wall of the grounds of a mental hospital that one very warm, sultry afternoon a motorist suffered a puncture. As he removed his jacket, rolled up his sleeves and began to get his tool-kit out of the boot his temper was not in any degree improved by the sight of one of the inmates of the institution watching him from over the wall with dull, vacant, but unwavering interest. Having got the car jacked up he removed the wheel plate which he laid face downward on the ground, and into which he carefully placed each of the four wheel-nuts as he unscrewed them. He then turned his attention to pulling off the wheel – a task which proved more difficult than he had anticipated. When at length it decided to come off it did so with a jerk and he found himself stepping back quickly to retain his balance. In doing so, needless to say, he put his foot on the edge of the wheel-plate and watched with fascination as the four wheel-nuts, one after the other, rolled down the camber and disappeared with a plonk through the grating down into the drain.

'Is there a garage hereabouts?' he enquired of his audience who had been following the course of events without any evidence of interest, let alone of sympathy. 'Doon that road,' pointing in the appropriate direction. 'Is it far?' 'Aboot a mile an' a hauf.' 'Well I suppose there's nothing else for it,' said the motorist resignedly, getting into his jacket. 'Here,' said the man across the wall, 'if you had three nuts wad that haud the wheel on till ye got to the garage?' 'Of course it would. But,' in a tone of exasperation, 'I don't have three nuts, have I?'

'Naw. But I was thinkin' if ye was to tak one nut aff each o' the other three wheels ye wad have three nuts.' 'Here, that's an idea,' said the motorist. Then turning to his technical adviser he said, I thought you fellows in there were supposed to be daft.' 'Ay, we're daft a' richt, but that doesna mean we've got to be stupid.'

To conclude the chapter I throw in the tale of the tailor's goose as an example of how a simple mind can contrive to avoid the howler.

The tailor could no longer iron his suits properly – his goose had packed it in. He decided he'd better have a new one – in fact he'd better have a spare as well just in case he was left in the lurch again. For what use is a tailor without his goose?

So he wrote to the manufacturers asking them to supply him with two tailor's geese. That somehow didn't look right, so he got a fresh sheet of paper and asked this time for a pair of tailor's gooses. That seemed definitely worse. He tried again, confining himself this time to the singular goose and ringing the changes on the position of the apostrophe in the 'tailor's'. Still no joy.

Inspiration came at length and he wrote asking for one tailor's goose. And then he added a postscript – 'On second thoughts you'd be better to send two.'

As a matter of interest do you happen to know what it ought to be? If not I imagine that the Irishman of today's jokes would call you a tailor's dummy!

CHAPTER TEN

AS MEAN AS GET OUT

Just as it is difficult to define what is so essentially funny about a drunk man, so there is no obvious reason why a mean person should be an object of mirth. The mean, penny-pinching cheese-parer could well evoke our pity, or even our derision, but why our laughter? As we watch him carefully bringing out his purse and studiously counting over his small change we may be forgiven for wondering what he gets out of life; but why should we find the picture so entertaining? Even when as in the classic picture the moths are seen flying away when the purse is opened – there is no obvious occasion for merriment.

Yet it is beyond question that manifestations of meanness are a fertile source of mirth. A whole department of fun – mainly of the picture post-card variety admittedly – has grown up around the Aberdonian, who has gained a worldwide reputation as the meanie par excellence. You have seen the picture of Aberdeen's main shopping street, not a soul in sight, carrying the caption, 'Flag Day in Aberdeen'. You may have heard that beneath the city's coat-of-arms is printed 'Bang went saxpence'.

You may have heard of the Aberdonian counting and recounting his change in the London store who, on being asked if his change was right, grudgingly conceded, 'Aye, but no' ony mair than right.' Or of the young husband spending his honeymoon alone in Rothesay who explained when asked about his wife's absence that he hadn't thought it justified the expense to bring her – you see she had been to Rothesay already. Or of that other native of the Granite City whose wife had died very suddenly in the course of the night and whose principal concern when morning dawned was to get instructions to the maid that there would be only one for ham and egg. Or, still worse, there was the Aberdeen lady who, when she wasn't doing anything, invariably shut her eyes – to save the wear and tear on her spectacles.

Now there is no doubt that the average Aberdonian is a hardy citizen – some of the qualities of his native grey granite seem to have rubbed off on him, he knows the value of his bawbees and he likes to get full value for each one of them, he is not the kind of person to whom to turn with some cock-and-bull hard-luck story in the hope of a lavish response. But, generally, speaking, I'm sure the Aberdonian is no less generous than other inhabitants of these islands. And certainly he can be much more generous than others I have known – without mentioning any place-names.

Before the discovery of North Sea oil revolutionised the whole economy of the north-east, Aberdeen was still considerably dependent upon the tourist industry and anxious to attract visitors – and their siller – to the city. I was of the opinion that each spring a public-relations officer was engaged for the sole purpose of producing a new dossier of jokes about mean Aberdonians. A judicious distribution of these among script-writers for comedians ensured for the northern city mention 'on the box' and in the music-halls throughout the country. Free advertising throughout the land is not to be sneezed at, and if by allowing potential visitors to have a laugh at you you fill your hotels and boarding houses then it's you who have the last and best laugh. The cost of advertising through normal channels is, for a careful man, no laughing matter.

I am further convinced of the truth of my theory because since the coming of the steady stream of oil men from Texas to fill every corner of every hotel the spate of Aberdeen jokes seems to have dried up. The Aberdonian is far too keen a business man to poke fun at himself unless a reasonable return is to be had from it. I wonder, parenthetically, whether there are not many in Aberdeen today who'd sacrifice some of the present prosperity for some of yesterday's laughs.

We still haven't answered the question as to what there is about meanness that's so terribly funny. The answer, I think, is that it's not the cheese-paring as such that inspires the laugh. Rather it is the kind of situation that the meanness can create that can be quite funny. For example, in the following tale of the young lovers it's not the fact of the fellow being so mean that triggers off the laugh, it's the length to which he carries his meanness and the gloriously unselfconscious way in which he is able to do it.

The lassie had just returned home after her first major day out with her new boyfriend. It was instantly clear to the discerning mother that the event had not been an unqualified success. A little questioning elicited the explanation that Jean had found him to be 'awful mean'. 'You know, mum,' she said, 'I got the impression that he grudged every penny he spent on me. He keeps his money in a purse and he counted it out so cautiously I was fair embarrassed. I'm never going to go out with him again.'

'If that's the way of it,' said the mother, 'the best plan would be for you to work out what he spent on you and go away round to his house and give it to him. You don't want him to be losing sleep over what he spent.' This was agreed, a note of outlays was prepared and this note put in an envelope along with the money.

It was Bob himself who came to the door. 'That,' said the young lady proferring the envelope, 'is the money you spent on me today. Mum said it wasn't fair to have you out of pocket on my account.'

'Och, Jean,' he said, taking the envelope, 'you shouldn't have bothered coming round specially with it tonight. It would have been time enough for you to give it to me next Saturday.'

In the following story the laugh comes from the fact that you are all prepared for a very grudging gesture of generosity by way of squaring the account – but not, surely, for one so mean as what actually occurs.

The Aberdonian and his London host were approaching the ticket machines at Piccadilly Circus Tube station. The host pushed forward, indicating that he would attend to this little item.

'Not at all,' said the man from the north, 'Ye'll dae nothin o' the sort. You paid for the dinner and you paid for the drinks, you bought the tickets for the theatre and you've just settled with the taxi-driver. No, no, you've done your share o' treatin'. We'll each just buy oor ain tickets for the Tube.'

Again in the following story it's not strictly the meanness that amuses us but the rather interesting way in which Greek meets Greek – even if separated by a generation.

The lawyer in the small Aberdeenshire town was increasingly aware of the fact that the step leading up to the front door of his office was wearing into a hollow. He was happy enough that other people's premises should present traps that led to broken bones that in turn gave rise claims that could even end up in profitable litigation in the Court of Session, but he had no desire to be himself involved at the receiving end of that kind of process.

So he called in the local mason and sought a price for cutting and inserting a new stone. The quotation when he studied it seemed excessive. When he remonstrated over this he was told that the cost of cutting and transporting from the quarry a new stone was not inconsiderable. 'Very well, then, my man,' he said to the mason, 'what is to prevent you cutting out the present stone, turning it over on to its other side and bedding it down again?' 'Man,' said the mason, 'that's a great idea. I never would hae thocht o' that. That way it would cost you only the price o' the labour.' He got the order to proceed.

After a little while the mason hurried excitedly into the office, 'It's no' goin' to dae. It'll no' dae at a'.'

'Why? What's gone wrong?'

'You're ower late. Yer faither thocht on it first.'

The following yarn is one of those that gains a good deal of its effect from the fact that the hearer has to fill in quite a bit of reasoning if the message it to get through – the kind of story that can leave the man who is a bit short on a sense of humour waiting for the rest of the tale. At the same time economy if carried to such a length could of itself be quite funny.

A doctor had spent the whole of his professional life in the one community where even during his lifetime he had already become something of a legend. This was not primarily because of his medical skill, but rather for two things – his longevity and his meanness. Beyond knowing that he must be a 'great age' nobody had a clue as to his date of birth; and as to the fortune which his habits of penury must have amassed, that could only be the subject of conjecture, but a vast deal of interested conjecture it did invoke.

When in the fullness of time he was gathered to his fathers, speculation ran high on both of these topics. The extent of his fortune, they all knew, would shortly be revealed in the press when the executors took confirmation of the estate. But they wouldn't have so long to wait for the answer to the question of his age, for would not that appear for all to behold along with his name on the coffin lid. But they were due a disappointment – the old chap had run true to form to the very end. As the mourners craned forward to read the age of the deceased they saw screwed on to the lid of the coffin a brass plate they had seen often before – it said, 'John Brown, Physician. Consults daily 11 a.m. and by appointment.'

Of all the Aberdeen stories I have heard – and I have heard a wheen – there is none that I like half so well as the following. The carefulness is not the real secret of the fun, but it does provide a backdrop for a highly entertaining incident to be played out. It also contains an element of the macabre which is characteristic of a vast deal of Scots humour.

An esteemed citizen of Aberdeen was lying close to death. Three of his friends were keeping vigil at his bedside, but when he fell into a coma they felt free to turn their chairs round to the fire and to turn their attention to making some tentative arrangements for the forthcoming interment.

'He's awfu' weel kenned,' opined the first friend, 'there's bound to be a lot of folk'll want to go to the funeral. I wad think we would need the hearse and maybe a dozen, or even fifteen cars.'

'Haud on a meenut,' said the second more cautious friend. 'We havena seen the colour o' his siller yet. I wadna want to go erin' a lot o' cars till we ken the kind o' money we've got to spend. Forbye,' he went on, his naturally parsimonious nature asserting itself, 'what wad we want wi' o' thae cars? If we had a hearse and mebbe four, or even five, cars for the kind o' auld bodies, the rest o' the mourners could perfectly well walk. It's nae distance to the cemetery – they would hardly be in the cars till they were oot o' them, onyway.'

Not to be outdone the third member chipped in, 'Weel if that's to be the way o't I think it wad be faur better juist to have the hearse an' let everybody walk – mak' it a proper auld-fashioned walkin' funeral. It's mony a day syne we had a thing o' that kind. I aye thocht it was a real nice solemn-like way for geein' a body a guid send-off.'

Unbeknown to the three planners the chap in the bed – the deceased designate as you might call him – had considerably recovered and had been taking a lively interest in what was afoot (or at least in who were to be afoot). The friends were a trifle surprised when their deliberations were interrupted by a voice from the bed, 'Nae sense throwin' awa' siller on a hearse. Rax me my troosers an' I'll walk tae.'

Thinking of this business of the macabre it would be hard to surpass the tale I'm about to recount. I'm sure the story does not belong to Aberdeen – it could well find a domicile in any country parish in Scotland. I have commented elsewhere on the fact that the Scot tends to be on speaking terms with the devil. In the same way he could be thought to be very much at home among graves, coffins, hearses and the like.

The local undertaker, walking down the street of his little town one fine morning, was joined by a citizen of some standing who, after the usual exchange of comments on the weather, the harvest prospects, the price of butcher meat, etc., remarked, 'Ye ken ye're the very man I was wantin' to see. Ye never seem to lift a newspaper these days but ye read aboot a sudden death. It gars ye think. It got me started puttin' some o' my affairs in order. Now what I was wonderin' was what would you charge for a coffin for a fella the likes o' me?'

The professional man eyed his prospective customer up and down measuring him with a kind of mental foot-rule, 'Aye, aye, ye would want elm of course, an' it wad need quality furnishing, an' it would have to be proper brass handles, an' a' nice-like – och well, for you, say something aboot eighty pounds – aye, or better be on the safe side an' say eighty-five – aye, that's it, eighty-five pound – an' that's for a freend.'

'Eighty-five pounds,' came the horrified reply, 'cannie man, cannie. That's an awfu' money for a bit box. D'ye ken what I'm gonna tell ye – I was talkin' to Geordie the joiner nae later than last week, an' he said he could chap me a bit box thegither for about twenty-five pound.'

'That'll be right enough,' conceded the mortician, 'he could chap you up a box nae bother for that money. But it wad never dae for the likes o' you. For one think it wad juist be in white pine. Your backside would be oot through it in nae time.'

While the as-mean-as-get-out joke has inclined to locate itself geographically in Aberdeenshire the attitude which it represents has its habitat socially among the farming community throughout the whole country. Again, of course, it is true that the men and women of the land can be as generous – if not more so – than their city neighbours. But somehow where money is in question they can be 'pretty careful'. This, I imagine, is due to a long tradition of having a rent to find come term day when what assets they had were in the form of grain or cheese or fattening beasts or the like and not always readily realisable.

The whole economy of agriculture has changed radically of recent years, but an attitude that has developed steadily over the centuries is not so easily altered. I remember a well-to-do farmer who, when approached about the possibility of taking out a covenant for a modest sum in favour of the kirk was utterly horrified – he could never tell, he said, from one week's end to the next, how he might be placed. And I'm sure he was being quite honest, if utterly inaccurate, when he said so.

I remember being present when a farmer was approached by a tinker in search for some food for his pony. He went away with some hay, some straw, some seconds of corn and a wheen of turnips worth in all quite a few pounds. And yet had he had the effrontery to ask for fifty pence he would, I know, have been chased off the farm – probably with a shot-gun to expedite the manner of his going.

Nowhere is this meanness more clearly manifested than in the farmer's attitude towards his worker. The trouble, I suspect, is that he finds himself in the position of having to part with siller – every week at that – and he understandably wants to see something happening by way of return. Holidays of all sorts and for whatever reason are anathema. Not all farmers are as bad as the man who, when approached by his ploughman to see whether he could have a half-day at Christmas to visit his grandchildren, replied, 'Get aff at dinner-time on Christmas Day? What'll ye be wantin' next? It's nae time since ye had to stop for the two minutes silence.'

It would probably be no more than a joke, but a joke with a pretty sharp edge to it when the dairyman slept in, appearing in the byre at 5.30 a.m. instead of 5 o'clock sharp and the boss greeted him, 'Hallo, what have you been daein a' forenoon?' One of my own dairy farmers used to tell me in all earnestness, 'I'm always up before four, but I never chap the boys till quarter past. It's nice, isn't it, to get a long lie.'

The following pair of stories illustrate quite vividly a frame of mind that wants full value for wages and no nonsense about it.

Throughout the short November day there had been a relentless sleety drizzle – not a downpour, but just rain without ending. From the first grey dawn the man with his pair of horses and his plough had traversed the field, back and forth, back and forth. The last of the light had now faded and he was stabling his beasts and bedding them down for the night, the while the water was running out of his own clothes.

He was passing the time of day with the boss who was sitting on the corn-kist watching the dripping harness being hung on its pegs. 'An awfu' day o' rain,' remarked the drookit ploughman.

'Aye,' agreed the farmer, 'a sair day for this horse and harness.'

And what do you think of this one?

It was one of those old-fashioned feeing fairs where servants were engaged for the ensuing six months. A farmer was telling a likely ploughman some of the many advantages of entering his employ. The servant, however, had his reservations and his own line of enquiry to follow.

'An, what,' he enquired, 'do you do when it's ower wet for plooin?'

The prospective employer stated after due deliberation that he could not, from his own experience, remember a day when it had been too wet to follow the plough, but that he supposed, were such a day to emerge, 'We could go oot an' cut hedges.' And if you can imagine the effect of swiping at a dripping hedge you will see what is meant by the phrase 'out of the frying pan into the fire'.

I like the story of the farmer who allowed his enthusiasm to carry him away to the point of committing the supreme act of generosity – to write out a blank cheque.

Father and son were returning from the Harvest Thanksgiving Service. It had been a good year and they had full barns for which to give thanks. 'I'll no say but what it's been a guid harvest,' conceded the farmer. 'I canna say I mind us hae' in' a better so far as the barley's concerned. An' we've got the tatties dug an' pitted in the best o' tid. No, I'm no' complainin'.'

Nothing was said for a while and then Father took up the tale afresh, 'I've been thinkin', Tammie, you've been a big help to me. If it hadna been for you we would never have got in the crop the way it is. One o' these days, as like as no', you'll be thinkin' o' gettin' married an' settin' up on yir ain, an' you'll be needin a pickle o' siller at your back.

'So what I've done here is I've written you out a cheque for a hunner pound.'

Taking the piece of folded paper from an inside pocket he solemnly handed it over. 'And if ye tak' my advice ye'll put it awa' in a safe place, an' if we have as guid a harvest next year you bring it back to me an' I'll mebbe sign it for you.'

Talking of a bumper harvest, there was one year I remember when things had gone really well for the farmers and record crops had been got in in the best of order. I was saying so to one of my farmers and suggesting he could have nothing to complain about this year. 'Oh aye we've had a guid hervest richt enough, but o' man it's ta'en an awfu' lot oot o' the grund.'

There are always the Unsatisfied, but there are always too the Unsatisfiable. I can conceive of no better way to close this chapter than with the tale of the man who earned – but never enjoyed – the wee hauf.

The lady had been to the auction-rooms and there had bought herself an old-fashioned sewing-machine. She engaged a porter to carry it home for her. The day was warm; the weight of the burden was considerable; the lady's house was quite a bit away and three flights up. Having got into the house the man laid his burden down on the floor and then wiped the sweat from his face, using for the purpose the lining of his bonnet, remarking the while that not only was it a warm job but that on a day like this it can fairly gi'e ye a thirst.

All solicitude, the lady having paid him his dues remarked, 'Perhaps you would care for an orange.'

'No, mistress, but thanks a' the same. I'm no' what you would say daft on fruit.' Then he added hopefully, 'No but what I'm thirsty richt enough.'

Looking round to ensure she was not overheard the lady enquired with a conspiratorial wink, 'Maybe you could manage a wee half.'

'Noo there's a thing I wadna' say no to,' said the delighted porter.

The lady went to a drawer whence she produced a knife with which she cut the orange in two.

To the proverb about never counting your chickens until they're hatched could be added a postscript: 'Never enjoy your wee-half until it's been wee-halved'.

CHAPTER ELEVEN

GLASGOW LAUGHS

THE CITY OF GLASGOW IS BLESSED with what is probably the finest and best-equipped hospital of its kind in the world. Its title is simply The Southern General Hospital, but typical of the city it is known generally as 'The Sufferin' General.'

In the course of our fairly extensive journeyings abroad (which, of course, includes England) I have come across the most contradictory opinions regarding the character of my native city.

The one extreme is represented by the example of a couple of very refined English ladies with whom we shared a table in St Andrew's Hospice in Jerusalem during a visit I paid there when Moderator of Assembly. Said one of the ladies to my wife at the breakfast table our first morning that we would, she expected, be based in Edinburgh. O no, Queenie explained, we were working from our normal home which was in Glasgow. 'That must be pretty grim,' was the instant response offered in tones of deepest sympathy. On being pressed for an explanation she said, 'Well, everyone knows about Glasgow with its violence and crime and all the rest of it. But I expect there must be quite nice parts to it too.' A positive curate's egg of a city!

The other side of the story was that in some of the most unikely places to which our Moderatorial travels took us we met people whose faces lit up at the very mention of Glasgow – they described it as the friendliest place they had ever known, going on, usually, to give details of kindnesses they had received when their travels had taken them there. It was in a lovely little hotel in Devon that our host flatly refused to charge for our night's stay – it was, he insisted, a small repayment for all that Glasgow had given him when the war had taken him there for a brief spell.

That views so contradictory should be held by different people must be capable of an explanation. That is so, and I think the explanation is very simple. On the one side you have those who are dependent on the media for what they know of our city while on the other side you have those who have enjoyed being there, of getting to know its people at first hand, of getting the feel of its life and character – in short of enjoying it.

Those whose knowledge of people and places comes from the media are one and all satisfied that 'Glasgow' is synonymous with violence and vandalism, drunkenness and gang fighting, foul language and still fouler deeds. If something defies description it surely had its origin on the banks of Clyde.

I imagine it is convenient for the media to equate habits with habitats. For oil read Aberdeen, for pomp and pageantry read Edinburgh, for all that is darkest in Presbyterianism read Stornoway, for Highland customs and costumes read the Braemar Gathering, for wickedness to the enth degree read Glasgow. Thus any mention of gang warfare sends the editor scurrying to his 'Glasgow' file to unearth some columns of type or some yards of tape connected with that city and its record of violent crime. The unhappy consequence of this is that those who don't know can be misinformed and those who ought to know better can begin to entertain doubts.

Even those most heavily prejudiced in its favour – me for instance – must agree that Glasgow has its share of the most disgraceful activities, but those who know the city best are quite convinced that, except on the television screen, they are not its most conspicuous characteristics. Indeed a television team that visited the city recently to get some clips of juvenile-delinquency-in-action had eventually to gather a bunch of kids and pay them a small sum to stage a set-to that could be filmed for inclusion in a stretch depicting life in Scotland's industrial capital.

It is not surprising that the more generous view of Glasgow is the one held by those with first-hand knowledge. In more than one place during my travels as Moderator I came across Europeans who had spent a spell in our city at some time during the war and who could not wait to tell me of incidents during their stay proving that Glasgow is the friendliest and kindliest place they had visited.

This, I am sure, is not the whole picture any more than is the other. But it is important to remember that so far as it goes it is a true picture.

For myself I would agree that the spontaneous generosity of Glasgow people has to be experienced to be believed, and while I would concede that we have our full share of violence and vandalism I would point to one of the principal characteristics of the Glasgow man – his wonderful sense of humour, for there is a type of fun that is somehow 'pure Glasgow', there are stories that couldn't possibly have their source anywhere else. This sense of humour has enabled him to see the laugh in many a situation that would fill others with dismay. Not least important it has enabled him to have a good hearty laugh at himself and feel and be the better for it.

In the eight hundred years of its history Glasgow, like Rabbie Burns, has had misfortunes great an' sma', but also, like the poet, it's had a heart abune them a'. In the days of the Depression in the 'thirties I've known Glasgow homes so low there literally wasn't a bite in the larder, but never so low they didn't put on the kettle when you called. I have known Glasgow people sore buffeted with sorrow and misfortune, but never so far down they couldn't raise a smile in answer to a joke. That use of humour as a defence against despair goes some way, it may be, to explain the peculiar nature of Glasgow fun.

As I have said there is a kind of joke that somehow proclaims itself as having had its source in Scotland's industrial capital, that might be thought to bear a label 'Clyde Built'. What are the characteristics of such a joke? For one thing it is earthy and that in two senses – first in the sense that there's no frilly nonsense about it, it's simple and straight to the point; secondly in the sense that it's blunt and down to earth, so that if it should happen to contain a reference to a spade that will surely be so called – if it is not referred to as a 'bloody shovel'. That is not to say that it is 'dirty' in the way much that passes for humour today in even the most respectable circles. Even when it could be called 'dirty' the Glasgow variety is good clean dirt and there's never a leer or a sneer or a snigger to it.

I should say too that the typical Glasgow joke has to it an element of simplicity – indeed it could often be described as 'stupid' in the same way (if not to the same offensive degree) as are many of the so-popular 'Did-you-hear-about-this-Irishman' tales that go the rounds today. It's an interesting fact, of course, that in these enlightened times the Irishman is about the only person to whom you can credit stupidity without danger of prosecution under race relations legislation, if not also of a payment to heal hurt feelings.

And then, of course, it's quick, and like most such humour it has a taste of acid about it – not enough to poison, just enough to flavour. For it's also a kindly humour – being Scots it's bound to be. The one thing which in my view distinguishes the sectarian bitterness on this side of the Irish Channel from that on the other is that here most people are able to relax a little, and smile, and even crack a joke about it. Now immediately you are in a position to see a problem as a subject of mirth – even of a constrained sort – you've got the measure of it. It's from those who take it all so deadly seriously that the troubles come, and the troubles can be serious enough in all conscience.

The same thing is true in respect of race relations, which in my corner of the city means essentially how to get on along with the largely Pakistani population upon whom in the earlier days we were utterly dependent for running our transport system. They do other things, of course, like being shopkeepers, nurses, doctors, professors, but until recently the average Glasow man envisaged his Asian neighbour as being in the green uniform of the transport service. These visitors to our city have become the subject of a positive anthology of jokes. Note that I say the subject – not the object – for that is a significant difference. Many of the tales could for all I know constitute an offence in terms of current legislation, but it would be indeed a pity were a prosecution to be brought, for all the jokes contribute to good relations and a kindly attitude. I'm sure one good joke helps more than half-a-dozen bad Acts of Parliament. It's fine to get it out of your system with a laugh – the laugh at least is better than the fine! (Forgive the pun.) On second thoughts a prosecution might be a good thing – it might well indicate just how unreal the whole affair is when reduced to its essentials.

There's something deeply touching and very understandable in the proposition of the chap who didn't want to offend the tender ears of a man of the cloth.

> The priest was sitting in the bus reading a book when he was joined by one a trifle under the weather. 'Guid evenin', Father,' the newcomer introduced himself. 'Good evening to you,' was the rather frigid reply.
>
> 'Sure an' it's been a lovely day, Father,' was the next attempt at cameraderie.' 'Yes, indeed, it has, my son.'
>
> 'You know, Father, I'm a very good Catholic. I come to Mass every Sunday, an' I niver miss confession. What's more, Father, I come of a good Catholic family – my sister's a nun. Yes, Father, my sister's a nun in the Convent of the Bloody Wounds of our Blessed Saviour Jesus Christ – if you'll forgive the language, Father.'

There's the tale of the Irishman who complained that his boss was a most unreasonable man for he had sent him for a colour television without without specifying what colour. Or that of the other Irishman who was buying nails and on being asked by the ironmonger how long he wanted them replied that he wanted them to keep. It's even said there was an Irishman who advertised a passport for sale 'owner going abroad.'

You could be excused, I think, for wondering how much of the stupidity was genuine and how much contrived in a situation of the kind represented here.

The letter bore the postmark of a town in the south of England where bishops are bishops and no nonsense about it. Which probably explains why it was addressed to 'The Bishop of Glasgow and Galloway, The Palace, Glasgow, N.B.'

In North Britain Their Graces tend to be held in rather less esteem – and this in turn probably explains why, when at length it reached its destination, the envelope had written across it, 'Not known at The Palace. Try The Pavilion.'

Quite a theatrical performance!

The homeliness of the true Glasgow joke comes out with especial force in this tale of the old priest who was getting hard of hearing and facing problems in consequence. It was proving of particular embarrassment to penitents who, while prepared to speak freely (within reason that is), of their deviations from the path of rectitude within the confidentiality of the confessional, resented proclaiming their misdeeds for the interest of all who might contrive to be within earshot. Representations were made to the old man on the subject.

'I tell you what,' he said, after due discussion of the subject, 'just write your sins on a slip of paper and pass it to me through the grille and this will do fine.' This proved an admirable system and business was soon restored to its normal brisk level. Until one day the old chap got a *billet-doux* that puzzled him. 'I'm afraid there's been a mix-up here, my daughter,' he whispered, 'this says, "Half-pound ham, packet semolina, plain loaf . . ." '

'Oh God,' came the anguished reply, in tones that even the deaf old priest could hear, 'Huv I no' went an' handed in my sins to the Co-operative!'

Which is rather of a piece with this other Glasgow tale.

The man had just come from a meeting at which he had heard a powerful address on the subject of Charity – the charity that gives all its goods to feed the poor. With the challenge of the talk still echoing in his heart he observed what was quite obviously something of a down-and-out loitering on the edge of the pavement. As he passed he slipped a pound into the stranger's hand. 'For charity,' he whispered. Some days later he happened to be in the same street when the same down-and-out came hurrying after him. 'Where have you been?' he panted as he caught up, 'I've been looking everywhere for you. Here's your winnings. Your horse came in twenty to one,' handing him his pound accompanied by four crisp new fivers.

Alongside the element of simplicity, and in strange contrast with it, there is a quality of sharpness and even of cunning in the

Glasgow character, and this too is reflected in the local humour.

The little chap was obviously to go far in the legal profession, such was his early grasp of the principle behind the plea of 'irrelevant and lacking in specification.' His mother was trying to persuade him to enjoy a plate of the most nutritious soup for which he seemed to have just no appetite. 'Come on now and sup it up,' she coaxed, 'it's lovely soup. I'm sure there are twenty boys in this street who would give anything to have a lovely plate of soup like that to come home to.'

With devastating cogency William replied, 'Name wan.'

A lawyer friend tells of the following incident.

The man had come into his office from the street and explained that he wanted to be defended on a criminal charge that was shortly to be served on him. After briefly narrating the circumstances surrounding his arrest he went on to say that, of course, he was pleading Not Guilty and that his defence would be one of alibi.

On being asked for the particulars of the alibi and the names of the witnesses who would testify to it he exclaimed, 'O, give me time. I havena got round to arranging all that yet. I'll give you a ring next week.'

It would be hard to beat the tale of the two Glasgow neds who had been stopped by a policeman. He was quite clear they had been up to no good, but he had no evidence to establish this, and the average Glasgow ned is well up in the rules of evidence. So he was asking them some questions, though it was clear he was making little headway. At length he said to the one. 'Where do you live, anyway?' Quick as a flash came the reply, 'No fixed abode.' 'And what about you?' turning to the other. 'I live up the stair frae him.'

The Glasgow man's skill at rigging the evidence (as a way of ringing the changes on arranging an alibi) is well brought out in the following tale from the high flats.

The tenant of a house on the nineteenth floor, answering a furious ringing of her doorbell, was confronted by her neighbour holding her head in a state of confused agitation. 'Oh Maggie,' she blurted out as soon as the door was opened, 'a terrible thing has happened an' I juist dinna ken what to do.' She went on to explain that she and her husband had been having a bit of a set-to.

He had been standing close by the open window, and when the disagreement got to the stage of fisticuffs she had got in with a playful push that caught him off his balance – and over the window he had gone so that now he was lying down there on the pavement. 'Oh what am I to do?' she wailed.

'There's only wan thing you can do,' said her resourceful friend. 'I'll away in and phone for an ambulance, and in the meantime you run away doon as quick as ever you can an' stick a wet chamois in his haund.'

Reference to the high flats brings to mind a story which I like very much – it manifests so many of the qualities of the humour of our city.

Two men had arranged to visit their aged sick friend who lived on the twenty-ninth floor of a high-rise tower. When they got to the entrance hall they discovered what is not unusual in such cases – the kids have to find some way of passing the time if they are to keep off the street – that the lifts were out of action. One of the would-be visitors was all for abandoning the mission. The other, made of sterner stuff, pointed out how desperately disappointed their sick friend would be after looking forward so much to seeing them.

'But how in all the world are we ever going to climb up twenty-nine floors?' protested Mr Faintheart, 'we'd be faur better juist to sclimb up Ben Nevis when we're at it.' 'Ach, don't exaggerate, it's no' as bad as a' that,' countered Mr Lightfoot. 'There's nae hurry an' we can take oor time.' Then he had a brainwave. 'I'll tell you what we'll dae – we'll stop on every landin' an' we'll take turn aboot o' tellin' a joke. That way we'll get oor wind back an' we'll never notice hoo faur it is.'

Mr Faintheart was not wholly convinced but he agreed it was essential that they leave no height unscaled, no joke untold, no avenue unexplored, in their attempt to fulfil their promised visit to their friend. So off they set on their merry, if not particularly speedy, journey. They had got as far as Floor 25 when Mr Lightfoot whose turn it was to purvey the mirth said, 'I've juist thocht o' something that's awfu' funny. You might no' juist see the joke at first, but the mair ye think aboot it the funnier it gets.'

'Come on then, tell us it,' said Faintheart.

'I'm no' sure you would maybe think it was funny. At least not right away.'

'Try me,' said Faintheart.

'Well,' said Lightfoot with a merry chuckle, 'It's juist dawned on me – we're up the wrang close.'

This business of being led up the garden path, as I've pointed out elsewhere, is a standard device for creating a laughable situation. Just when you think you know what the whole thing's about and can yourself supply the missing line you find yourself presented with a totally different last line. Here is an entertaining instance – who could have would have expected this story to end as it does. And once again the earthiness is so much in the idiom of Glasgow.

The Glasgow man was explaining that he knew of a pub in the east end of the city where you could get 'a pint of beer, a pie, and a woman all for a pound.' His friend refused to believe that under conditions of spiralling inflation – not to mention V A T – such generous terms could anywhere be obtained – 'it's juist no' possible.'

'O but it's true – it's nae carried story. I've been an' I've had it for myself.' 'Well if you put it that way it must be true enough. But at that money there canna be muckle meat in the pie.'

Many entertaining exchanges have been overheard – or more exactly perhaps – have been alleged to have been overheard on the city bus. This may be an appropriate point to tell of a bus incident that illustrates the essential kindliness of Glasgow relationships.

The Sikh bus conductor, magnificent in his great white turban, went to great trouble to help the old lady off the vehicle, taking her by the arm as far as the pavement. 'Thank you very much, young man,' she said, 'that was most kind of you.' And on a note of real solicitude she added, 'And I hope your head will soon be better.'

To return, though, to the overheard conversation, there is the story of the girl not too well up in her geography that shows how remarkably realistic can be the attitude of the Glasgwegian. The admixture of Celtic in their blood may tempt him to be a poet, but at heart they are a pragmatist every time.

> Two girls were sitting together on the top deck of a city bus. 'Whaur did ye get to for your holidays this year, Jessie?' the one enquired. 'Ach we took a notion we wad like to go to Majorka. It was a' right.'
>
> 'Ay, Majorka. There's a wheen o' folk go tae Majorka thae days. Whaur exactly is Majorka?'
>
> 'How the hell wad I ken? We flew.'

Well, you must admit once the plane has taken off, circling the airfield a couple of times, you can't be expected to know even in what direction you are travelling.

Or what of this gem of condensed logic! The subject was tastes in food. Said the one, 'See fish: see Nella's new boy friend: he doesna like fish.' A type of syllogism unknown to the masters of formal logic.

Here's one that might be entitled 'Getting your Priorities Right.' It so clearly reflects an attitude to life and its responsibilities, and one not unknown in these days of the Welfare State – one, some would say, begotten of the Welfare State.

> Said the lassie to her friend sharing a seat on the top deck, 'Did you hear that Jessie Wilson's gettin' married next week? Quite a splash they're havin'?' 'Naw, I never heard. Who's she gettin' married on to?' 'Yon big fella Willie Broon. You're bound to ken him – she's been goin' wi' him steady for weeks noo.'
>
> 'Ay I ken him fine. But I didna ken he had a job.'
>
> 'Naw, nether he has. But he's a rare dancer.'

The Welfare State, it might be added, has produced attitudes even more extravagant than that – witness the following cross-talk. 'It's terrible what they do to you at the housing department. They've just put us into a split new house at Drumchapel, and do you know what I'm going to tell you, there's not a single stick o' furniture in it. An' no' a pot or a pan. You know this – we've all to sit on auld orange-box when we're we're watching the colour television. It's certainly nae encouragement to a body.'

The ready wit and the plain unvarnished approach to every situation are both to be seen in this tale from the city's tenements that are disappearing so fast.

The tradesman was busy putting a coat of black paint on the railings in the back-court of a city tenement when an upstairs window was thrown open and a woman shook out a duster over the precise area of his activities. Scarcely had he finished making good the damage done to his handiwork when again the window opened and this time a rug was shaken. 'Look here, mistress,' the exasperated workman shouted up, 'you shake wan ither thing ower that windae an' I'll come up an' I'll pent yer backside for ye.'

'Will ye, though,' came the contemptuous reply. 'Fancy!'

'Naw,' replied the man with the brush, 'juist plain black.'

A tale that is tremendously in character as 'pure Glasgow' was told in my hearing by one who is now a high-ranking member of the police force. Years ago, when a constable on the beat, he had occasion to visit a house on the top floor of a tenement in Garngad fairly early in the morning of a desperately cold winter's day. On his way down the stair he passed two women in dressing-gowns and carpet-slippers forming an orderly queue outside the W C on the half-landing. By way of something to say he remarked that it was 'a right cold stand' they were having this morning. 'It's all that,' replied one of the women, 'but at least the seat'll be nice an' warm.'

No matter to what department of humour you turn you are sure to find a story with an ecclesiastical slant. I like this one that could be entitled 'Whom the Cap Fits'.

It was a famous kirk and he was a preacher of some renown. People were queuing up for his evening services. One Sunday evening, preaching to the usual packed congregation, the minister was distracted by the sight of a young couple in the front of the gallery who were so busy making eyes at one another they were oblivious of everything he was saying. It got on his nerves a bit so that he paused in his discourse to say that there was a young couple in the Church clearly more interested in one another than in the sermon and that he would be glad if they would come to the vestry for a moment at the close of the service.

The service was over and the minister had got out of his robes when the beadle came into the vestry. 'What am I to dae wi' them?' he asked. 'To do with whom?' countered the minister who had completely forgotten about the incident.

'It's that couple ye said were to come an' see you after the service.' 'O yes, just show them in.' 'Show them in,' said the beadle. 'There's a line o' them stretchin' frae here right on to the street.'

There's a nice quality too in this tale of the haircut.

Fashion had got around to dictating a change in hair styles for boys from long ringlets to short-back-and-sides. The schoolboy explained his wants to the barber who got busy on his mammoth task. After a while he remarked, 'So you're a High School boy.'

'That's right,' said the lad, 'but how did you know?'

'I've just come on your bunnet,' said the man with the clippers.

And this one about selling records and breaking records is rather good is it not?

The lady phoned the record shop to enquire about a disc she was wanting to buy. By an unhappy chance she had been connected to the wrong number so that instead of speaking to the record salesman she was conversing with the local plumber.

'Do you happen,' she asked, 'to have "Ten Little Fingers and Ten Little Toes in Alabama"?'

'I'm sorry, Madam, I don't,' replied the somewhat-taken-aback plumber. 'But I've got a wife and fifteen weans across in Clydebank.'

The prospective customer was much interested. 'Is that so?' she said. 'I didn't know about that. Is that a record?'

'I'm no' sure aboot it bein' a record,' modestly replied the father, 'but it's certainly well above the average.'

Sometimes when Glasgow people climb up the social ladder a bit they affect a peculiar accent known locally as 'pen-loaf' or 'Kailvinsaide' – they refer to their city as 'Glesgow' and generally they monkey about with the quality of vowel sounds. It could be argued that they do less hurt to true vowel values than do the official news-readers and others on the media; but that, I agree, is a serious charge and it would be quite inappropriate to pursue a serious charge in a work on humour. It is said, incidentally, that a medical student from this stratum of Glasgow society on being asked what he would do with a headache replied without hesitation that he would fry it with chips. Funny as that may be it's no more entertaining than listening to an announcer trying to pronounce a word like 'impasse' in a way that will incorporate both Parisian French and BBC English. And as for 'entrepreneur' – it produces a kind of lockjaw. One can begin to understand the Frenchman who complained that we pronounced the name 'Marjoribanks' as 'Chumley', but who gave up completely when he saw outside a theatre – 'Cavalcade – pronounced Success'.

The point I was trying to make before I allowed myself to be diverted is that the Glasgow veneer is generally pretty thin and brittle and won't stand up to much strain, as is illustrated in this cliff-hanger.

> It was a morning of keen frost after rain, and the roads – even in the city centre – were highly treacherous. At the central bus station information regarding arrivals and departures was being dispensed over the loud-speaker system by a young lady in accents so polite as to be quite untrue.
>
> Until, that is, she reached the middle of one announcement.
>
> It began in polished syllables, 'The 7.45 bus from Kilmarnock now approaching Number Three Pletform' . . . and then in more natural if less polished tones . . . 'is comin' in sidieways!'

Vividly I remember an occasion when we were presented with the two tongues antiphonally.

> The occasion was some kind of open-air Scout show in which a pageant was being acted out by the boys in the arena, the commentary being 'spoken' and the boys directed by one and the same young lady officer from a tent surmounted by a loud-speaker. Their theme was Saint George and the Dragon.
>
> Unfortunately no-one had warned the lady that when you are holding a microphone close to your mouth everything you say comes over – not just the bits you had intended for broadcasting. And so we in the audience were treated to something like the following, 'The lovely maiden was about to be sacrificed to the dragon when Saint George – whaur is that boy! For goodness sake

153

tell him to get awa', oot – came forth to do battle with the terrifying creature – o heaven help us he's left his sword – which for so long had held the country in terror – ay you run awa' efter him wi' it' . . . and so on. It was far and away the best Scout show I had attended for years.

The popular Glasgow theme of the plain man scoring off his pen-loaf cousin was exploited with considerable effect in a radio series of long ago – the M'Flannels – which provided one of the most successful exercises of this sort since J J Bell immortalised the Glasgow child, 'Wee Macgreegor'. *The Sunday Post* series of cartoons on 'Oor Wullie' and 'The Broons' are in the same tradition.

The following bus yarn definitely belongs to that family, even if to a different branch of the same.

A number of people had swarmed on to the bus at the stopping-place and the conductress was busy counting the number unable to find seats on the lower deck. The total came to six, the last to be counted a very stout citizeness of homely appearance. 'You will have to get off,' the conductress informed her in extremely polite but not any less firm tones. 'I'm only allowed five standing passengers.'

With a very bad grace the stout one returned to the pavement, the bus moved off, and the clippie went to collect fares on the upper deck. The bus meanwhile was halted at traffic lights about thirty yards away from the stop. Seeing her opportunity the stout one covered the distance with remarkable agility, rejoined the bus and pushed her way inside.

A few minutes later the conductress came down the stairs and was appalled to find her friend. 'I thought I told you we took only five standing passsengers,' she assailed the offender. 'Five,' she repeated, and to drive home the point the more emphatically she held out the fingers of one hand and spelled out five – f i v e.

'Sure you're a right clever wee bitch,' said the stout one, 'ye're guid at the coontin' an' ye're guid at the spellin'. Noo let's hear ye try to spell 'cahootchie.''

It's that plain down-to-earth quality in the Glasgow man's outlook upon life and all its affairs that enables him to deal devastatingly with the pretentious and the precious. The tale I've just narrated about the spelling contest on the bus illustrates the point, but perhaps it is brought out with even greater pungency in the story of the Glasgow couple who were so proud of the fine match their daughter had just made – her husband was 'in the timber and fruit business'. 'Aye,' said the unimpressed neighbour, 'that'll be right. You see, he sells toffee-apples.'

Or, in the identical vein there's the story of Mr and Mrs Two-up-left who were making such a fuss over the fact that their son had just become engaged to a girl in the top social bracket – 'her people are in iron and steel, you know.' When Mrs One-up-right related this item to her husband his comment was, 'Ay, her mither stays in an' does the ironin', while her faither gaes oot and does the stealin'.'

It's the application of this down-to-earth quality to certain types of situation that brings out the element of the macabre so typical of Scottish humour. Naturally enough the fun of Glasgow contains many examples of this.

The grim realism of the Glasgow man when applied, for example, to a funeral can itself be quite blood-curdling. It was, of course, a Glasgow man who explained to his fellow-mourners, 'I'm to be MC at the funeral, for, you see, I'm a first cousin of the corpse.'

Or again there was the Glasgow woman who was admiring the mortician's handiwork in the laying out of her late husband. 'Yes, indeed,' she said, 'he's looking just beautiful.' And she added, 'You know, that holiday we had last month must have done him an awful lot of good.'

Then there was the other Glasgow widow who was entertaining in the kitchen some friends who had dropped in to offer their condolences on her recent bereavement and who were extolling the many virtues and excellences of the deceased whom they insisted on referring to as 'him that's lying through yonder'. After a while the widow said to her small son, 'Bobbie, run away through to the room and make sure it's your father that's lying there.'

A minister friend of mine had, a number of years ago, come to a Glasgow parish and found himself conducting a funeral at which he knew no one.

The company, as was not unusual in those days, were standing around the coffin which rested on trestles in the middle of the little sitting-room, and they were awaiting the arrival of some relative before the service could start. By way at once of easing the tension and of learning something about the late lamented the minister whispered to his neighbour, 'What occupation did the late Mr M'Whaggle follow?' Apparently he had directed his question to the inevitable 'stranger in these parts'.

But Glasgow people are nothing if not keen to be helpful. So the stranger in a loud voice asked the man at the head of the coffin, 'What trade was the corpse, Tammie – the minister wants to know.'

I remember myself once in one of these tiny tenement rooms as we all stood around the coffin in a silence that was becoming trying in the extreme, waiting for some late arrival. The electric light flickered (the curtains were always tightly drawn on such occasions) and as this happened the tension was broken by a tiny voice which piped up, 'Gas is needin' pennies.'

If I may move from funerals to weddings (a common enough transition for the minister of a down-town city parish) I should like to put on record this tale told by a city colleague.

The minister had a visit to his vestry one night from a couple neither of whom had any Church connection, who said they had come 'to see about getting married.' My friend told them all about what they needed to do in advance and then ran through the various elements of the service, concluding by taking them into the church to show them where everyone stood – and so on.

As they moved back towards the vestry the minister got out his diary and asked when exactly the wedding was to be.' 'O,'replied the bridegroom elect, 'we've nothing fixed yet – we're just looking round to get quotations.'

May I be allowed to end this group with a really silly yarn – which for all its apparent stupidity may not be a hundred miles from the mark.

Two Glasgow women were looking forward with keen antici-pation to the horror film they were on their way to see. As they got off the bus outside the picture-house the one said, 'Tina, you run across to the paper-shop an' get a packet o' fags an' I'll slip into the chemist's here an' get a bottle o' tranquillisers – they tell me it's an awfu' good film.'

I spoke earlier about the matter of race-relations and of how these have affected a city where the running of the transport system was to all intents and purposes dependent upon Pakistanis. These same Pakistanis are steadily establishing themselves as the shopkeepers of the city – between bus shifts, that is. There are countless jokes about 'the Pakis', most of them good-natured. Indeed I am sure it is in this way that Glasgow has reacted to and come to terms with a situation which in some other parts of the country has led to hostility, bitterness, and even bloodshed.

A fairly sharp edge is to be found to this tale, even if it's still a kindly enough crack. In any case it could well be argued that the joke is not all at the expense of our visitors.

The recent arrival from Bangladesh was having explained to him by a countryman longer established in these parts the various and varied benefits provided by the Welfare State. Not surprisingly he was incredulous. In particular he found it difficult to believe that a nation, however generously disposed to its own nationals, would be prepared to extend these benefits to newcomers to its shores immediately on arrival.

'You mean,' he said, 'people like us, we get these things an' we no' pay for them – people from Bangladesh like us?'

'Yes,' his friend reassured him, 'it's only for us that they are given. What it say on the envelope in which they come is 'OHMS' and what that means is 'Only for Hindus, Moslims and Sikhs.''

East and west meet in a most interesting confrontation in the following highly typical Glasgow story.

The Pakistani conductor was remonstrating with a Glaswegian slightly under the influence who was insisting on boarding a full bus. 'I tell you,' he said, 'I am jam-packet foo, you must wait for the next bus.' (It is quite remarkable even if readily understandable

how very idiomatic can be the language spoken by these strangers.)
Still the Glasgow man pushed and threatened. 'I tell you,'
reiterated the man in green, 'you cannot get on this bus. I am
sorree – vair sorree, but I am jam-packet foo.'

To which the Glasgow man ungraciously replied, 'I don't give a
damn what yer name is, I'm gettin' on your bus.'

This matter of the kind of English which foreigners speak being
determined by the district in which they have lived and learnt the
tongue is quite inevitable where people are starting from scratch
and picking up what they hear. It's different, for example, with
those who come over from the continent with a basic knowledge
of the language acquired from books at school. The latter will
surely become slightly corrupted after a sojourn in a place like
Glasgow, but they will never share the proficiency of those who
learn *viva- voce* from scratch.

The point is neatly made in a tale I sometimes recount.

It was at the time when the Erskine Bridge was being built on
the lower reaches of the Clyde. I was trying to get to the village of
Old Kilpatrick – not an easy thing at that time, for the old road
pattern had been abandoned and the new one was not yet
established. I had been back and forward a couple of times on the
main road without any success in finding my slip-road. Seeing a
man working at the roaside I stopped and asked him for directions.

Immediately the man looked up I realised he was a stranger to
our shores. Not that that need have surprised me – do not we
always pick on a 'stranger' when we want to ask directions! In this
case, however, my man was well informed and with a degree of
precision equalled only by his courtesy he told me precisely how to
reach my destination.

I was about to drive off with the usual cursory word of thanks
when I bethought me that something more elaborate was called
for in the name of race relations. So having thanked him I went on
to ask whether he had been long in Scotland. 'I been 'ere more
than a year,' he responded. 'And are you liking it?' I asked. 'Vair
much, I like it vair much. All are so vair kind.' I said I was
delighted to hear that and went on to add, 'You come from India,
I think.'

'No,' he expostulated, 'I not come from India – the gentleman who teach me English, he come from India.'

It's an odd thing that a local phrase, or even a local pronunciation which we accept without raising an eyebrow when heard on the lips of a local man can sound quite outrageously funny when coming from a stranger. The difference between the vernacular and the copy-book versions can land the visitor in all sorts of unforseen difficulties – as this makes obvious.

A Pakistani had served his probationary period as a conductor on the Glasgow buses and was, as it were, sitting his orals with a view to moving on to the establishment. He had satisfactorily answered a number of questions about routes etc when the examiner said, 'Now tell me this, if a big fight were to flare up on your bus with knives flashing and the rest what would you do?' 'I would close the doors and would instruct my driver to proceed vair fast to the nearest pollis-office.'

'Very good. And if a woman on your bus said she was pregnant and felt her pains coming on?' 'I would instruct the driver to telephone for an ambulance.'

'Very good. One final question. What would you do if you couldn't get the fare?'

'I would just have to go for my holiday on the first fortnight in August,' was the resigned reply.

The following tale – which I like very much – has all the stupidity you could expect in a good Glasgow joke, and it also has that delightful quality of holding the Glasgow man up as an object of mirth no less than his Pakistani brother.

It was obvious that the young man from Pakistan was new to these parts as he presented himself at the Glasgow transport garage to offer his services as a driver. It was obvious too, however, that he was a most competent driver. So they fitted him out in a uniform and told him to report for duty at 6.30 on the following Monday morning.

Monday duly arrived, as did the driver looking very trig in his kit. The duty inspector took him along and showed him his bus, gave him a note of his route and left him to it. Some little time later the inspector was horrified to see the bus exactly as he had left it except that the engine was now idly ticking over. Pushing open the door he saw the driver sitting at the wheel with that look of infinite patience that we associate with the orient.

'What's keepin' you?' demanded the inspector. 'I wait for my conductor,' said the man at the wheel. 'Dae ye no' ken this is a one-man bus – you don't get a conductor.' The eastern face betrayed the faintest suggestion of surprise. 'And what do we do about the fares?' he enquired.

'Look,' said the inspector, fast losing patience, 'how often do I have to tell you, this is a wan-man bus. You drive the bus, you draw in the fares, you give out the tickets. Noo do you understand! Juist hurry up an'get your bus awa' oot o' here.'

The bus duly departed, but it had not been gone any time when an S O S was received to send out a break-down wagon, there had been an accident. The inspector went out with the wagon and, arrived at the scene, found his bus neatly wedged into a shop-front, surrounded by ambulances, the Fire-Brigade, police cars, stretcher parties, the lot.

Standing nearby on the edge of the kerb, still wearing that look of infinite patience, stood his driver. Going over to him the inspector said, 'Nameo'goad' (he was a Glasgow man was the inspector) 'Nanameo' goad' what's happened here?'

'How do I know?' responded the driver, shrugging his shoulders. 'When it happen I am up on top deck taking the fares.' He rattled his bag to prove how successful he had been.

It's just a story!

CHAPTER TWELVE

TOO UTTERLY RIDICULOUS

WHAT IS THE CONNECTION BETWEEN fun and fact? Need there be any correspondence between them?

It is not unusual to commend a joke by prefacing it with the assurance '. . . and what's more this is absolutely true.' You may even go so far as to forswear yourself with some such declaration as 'and as sure as I'm standing here I actually saw it happening.' While not prepared to go so far as that you may avail yourself of the device of telling the tale in the first person as though it were an autobiographical anecdote (an effective way of telling any story) for in this way the impression is clearly given that it's bound to be absolutely true.

I do not myself see that an incident is any funnier because it represents fact rather than fiction. For it is a particular arrangement and concentration of circumstances that creates the amusing situation and whether or not such a grouping of events ever occurred should make no difference to the entertaining aspect. I would agree that something is gained by the idea that the incident, though it did not actually occur could perfectly well have happened – that even if it's not true it at least conforms to the pattern of reality. A tall yarn is all right so long as it reaches the height of stupidity.

There is a brand of humour where the incident related could not by any stretch of the imagination be true and yet the tale itself is highly entertaining. The events are too utterly ridiculous ever to have occurred and yet the story can raise a hearty laugh. The element of fantasy is so great as to become itself part of the joke. I quote the following as an example.

> She was one of the grocer's regular customers and on every visit
> she bought some tins of 'Cheetie-pus', that much advertised brand

of cat-food 'champion breeders use no other'. One day the grocer remarked that she must keep a lot of cats to judge by the number of tins she got through in a week. 'No,' she said, 'we don't have any cats. It's my man – he fair enjoys it in the sandwich for his piece.'

The grocer had misgivings about this type of menu, but he contented himself by asking from time to time about her husband's health. He was not in the least surprised when one day in answer to his usual question when she said that her man was in hospital. 'It'll be his stomach, I suppose,' he hazarded.

'No,' she replied, 'his stomach's fine, it's his back he's hurt. You see, he fell off the roof.'

The grocer expressed condolence and wondered what her man had been doing on the roof. 'You know,' she said, 'it's a funny thing but for a while he's been acting awfu' queer. At first he got that after coming in from his work and had his supper he wad sit and stare into the fire – ye couldna get a word oot o' him. In fact you could hardly get him to move. Then this last week or two he's got that when it came bed-time, instead of taking off his clothes he wad go oot an' climb onto the roof. An' now he's fell aff an hurt his back. I canna think what's come ower him.'

The grocer didn't venture a suggestion, though, if pressed, he could have.

Now I'm sure that nobody hearing that yarn is taken in for one solitary moment by the business of the woman and her sandwich-filling; and even if anyone were credulous to that extent their confidence must inevitably be shaken by the picture of the man gazing into the fire before he began climbing on to the roof. Yet the progression of his man-to-cat transmigration seems realistic enough. It's what might be seen as a true sequence set within a false context and that I believe is where the secret of its humour lies, for believe it or not, there are those who see it as an extremely funny story.

The same considerations apply in the case of this incredible story. You couldn't possibly believe it, yet the string of events piece together convincingly enough. We've all known drivers nearly, if not quite, as clueless.

'You'll be for Brighton as usual this summer?' said Smith to his friend Brown when he met him one fine spring day. 'No,' replied Brown, 'we thought we should give Brighton a miss this year. We're planning to take the car across the Channel and have a fortnight motoring on the continent. We thought it would be a complete change.'

This was dramatic news indeed, for Brown's timidity at the wheel was well known to all his friends – no-one had ever been known to accept a lift from Brown a second time. 'Will it not be a bit of an adventure taking the car? All this keeping to the right and so on?' asked Smith. 'You mean you've got to drive on the right hand side of the road on the continent?' Smith confirmed that this was so. Brown expressed surprise and not a little alarm. He indicated the whole project might have to be reviewed in light of this new information.

It was some months later that the pair met again. 'How did the continental holiday get along?' enquired Smith.

'We didn't go. We just went back to Brighton,' replied Brown. 'Come to think of it,' he went on, 'it was you who put us off the notion. You remember you told me about this keeping to the right. Well, I thought I'd better put in a bit of practice. So I tried it for the next couple of days. No thank you. Yon's positively dangerous. No wonder there's a lot of accidents on the continent.'

There are times when the incredible story achieves its laugh from the fact that there is a non-sequitur so outrageous as to be instantly repudiated as false – we just won't believe that anybody could be as stupid as all that.

'I'm awfu' worried,' said the Glasgow woman to her neighbour when they met on the stairhead. 'It was yesterday forenoon about eleven o'clock that I gave my man a pound and told him to go down the street and get me a cauliflower, an' I've never seen hunt or hare of him since. I'm gettin' real worried. What can hae happened to him?'

'Dae ye tell me that,' said her neighbour in tones of shocked incredulity, 'that's a terrible thing to happen.'

'But what am I to dae?'

'There's only one thing ye can dae – ye'll juist need to open a tin o' peas.'

I rarely wear a coat even on a cold winter's day. And this can cause difficulty when I am visiting someone, for on my departure my host can be counted upon to get worried about what he has done with the garment. On being assured that there was no such garment he expresses surprise at my habit (if I may be excused a cheap pun). By way of explanation I usually recount that on the night of my induction to my first parish someone walked into the vestry and stole my split-new winter overcoat. I go on to say that I there and then resolved that no-one would ever come that one with me again – hence my condition of abject and pitiful coatlessness.

I cannot say my hearers ever show much sign of being convinced. But the reasoning is surely sound enough and I have a very good precedent in the following anecdote.

The two miners were admiring the likely-looking whippet pup which one of them was proudly displaying. Her virtues were being fully rehearsed.

'I had a bit of trouble with her for a while,' the owner admitted and went on to tell that she had been forming a bad habit – instead of running to the door when she wanted out, she slipped through to the sitting-room and made herself comfortable under the sofa.

His friend sympathised with him. That, he claimed, was a habit which if once formed it was near impossible to cure.

'Aha, but I cured it all right,' said the owner. 'Simple enough too. I just sawed the legs off the sofa.'

A few years ago it was my privilege to represent the Church of Scotland at Montreal at the Centennial Assembly of the Presbyterian Church of Canada. In course of acknowledging the welcome extended to us I remarked that I was Clerk of what is alleged to be the biggest presbtery in the world, but that we in Scotland are not so profoundly impressed as are some people by sheer size. By way of illustration I told the story of the tourist from Inverteenie.

It was four years later on a visit to Vancouver that the tale was recounted to me – remarkably accurately – as having been of my own telling. From all of which I concluded that the story must have travelled fairly extensively. It would seem, therefore, to be worth recording.

The man from Inverteenie had been visiting friends in Canada and they had been showing him some of the more spectacular wonders of that great land. He had not been so impressed as they felt the circumstances merited. Always he had contrived to think of something in Scotland of comparable significance if not of equal size.

So one day they took him to Niagara Falls and as they gazed at the amazing spectacle of the thundering waters the host said 'Well, Tom, I bet you haven't anything back home in little old Scaw'land that's anything like that.'

'No,' conceded Tom, 'we've naethin' just like that. But I tell ye what, we've an awfu' guid plumber in Inverteenie that could mend it for you.'

I've a horrible suspicion that I have told that story already and if so I can only crave your indulgence. In any case it's worth two laughs, so enjoy the second one and hurry on to laughters new.

For here's another yarn, equally ridiculous if taken literally, but no less funny if taken (as a joke should always be) with a peppering of salt – if one may mix one's condiments. If it needs a title that could be 'The Tale of the Parrot and the Coalman'.

The Coalman knocked at the door. A queer kind of noise bade him, 'Come in, come in!' The Coalman opened the door and looked in to find the house empty except for the Parrot which, on seeing his black face, squawked over and over again, 'Ten bags an' the money's on the dresser.' Clearly coal was expected, equally clearly money to pay for it was laid out on the dresser. So the Coalman carried up the bags. Shutting the door of the cellar he went across to check that the money was on the dresser. Still the Parrot croaked on, 'Ten bags an' the money's on the dresser.'

'My, Polly,' said the Coalman emptying the money into his pouch, 'but you're a rare speaker.'

'Ay,' replied the Parrot, 'I'm a rare counter too. We'll have another two bags.'

It would be very nice indeed to think that the following story was true. I won't say I doubt it, for I haven't the slightest doubt but that it's a product of the imagination – and of a fertile imagination at that. The peculiar feature of this joke is that the humour arises from the clash occurring when a sound enough piece of reasoning is met within a context which if not manifestly false is at least most unconventional. But then the very phrase 'honour among thieves' is essentially a contradiction, so it's not to be wondered at if it turns out to be the father of contradictions.

The minister had spent some years as a prison chaplain, so when a visitor was ushered into his study at the manse and was known to him as a member of his former flock-within-bars he prepared himself to repel what he envisaged as the inevitable 'touch' that would follow the equally inevitable ingratiating introduction.

Sure enough the conversation began with a most fulsome tribute for all the chaplain had done for this man when he had been 'inside', what it had meant to him, how significantly it had contributed to his turning over a new leaf, how deeply he had appreciated it, how very much he felt in debt. All this was following a standard pattern and seemed to be providing a suitable lead-in for the suggestion that the entire work of regeneration might now be crowned by the loan of a fiver.

Instead, however, of pressing on logically to this conclusion the grateful one explained that the sole object of his visit was to see whether there was anything he himself could do for the minister by way of a small acknowledgement for all the many kindnesses received.

'But that is most generous of you,' said the man of God, 'that speaks of true reform. I cannot at the moment think of anything you could do for me. But that you should have so much as thought of such a thing cheers me more than I can find words to express. No, thank you very much: I cannot think of anything. But it was indeed good of you to come.'

'Oh I don't know about that,' replied the penitent one, 'I'm sure there must be something I could do for you – at least for a start I could fix your electric meter.'

The mere mention of ministers has the effect of turning my mind to stories with the kirk as a background. The following is incredible and yet very sound in its sequence. Some might even wonder whether it was all that incredible! Some might even be able to parallel it from the pages of recorded history.

The Kirk Session of the country parish of Kirkmeanie had resolved to add to its number and in consequence approach was being made to one or two likely people who might be prepared to act as elders. The Session Clerk, who was a bit of a wag, was trying to persuade one none-too-enthusiastic countryman to consider sympathetically the idea of becoming an elder. He outlined the various duties. 'You should think aboot it, Erchie,' he concluded, 'ye ken ye get a new suit o' claes afore the March communion an' a pound-note oot o' the plate each Sunday you are on duty at the door.'

Impressed by these generous terms Archibald decided to let his name go forward and in due course he was welcomed into the ranks of the Session and took up the various duties involved, which he performed faithfully and well.

Close on a year had passed when one day Archie approached the Session Clerk. 'I was thinkin', Willie, it was mebbe aboot time I was gettin' measured for that new suit o' claes you said I was due come the spring.'

'What suit?' enquired the bewildered Clerk.

'D'ye no' mind? When you asked me to join the Session ye said there was a new suit o' claes before the March communion an' a pound note oot o' the plate ilka Sunday you were on duty at the kirk door.'

'Oh that. That was juist a joke,' said Willie. 'If you want a new suit o' claes, Erchie, I doot ye'll be like the rest o' us and buy it yersel'.'

'So that was the way o't – it was just a joke,' said Archibald. 'Well, let me tell you this, the pound-note has been nae joke – I've seen to that.'

This tale of the child awarded the fancy name in baptism is too tall by half to be credible. It would be impossible for anyone with any experience of such situations to find it other than hilariously funny. 'There but for the grace of God . . .' some of us ministers might find ourselves muttering.

It was a Church Extension charge situated in the midst of a vast new housing estate and the one department in which it could incontestably be said to be flourishing was in the dispensation of baptism. On the first Sunday of each month the sacrament was publicly administered and consistently involved having between ten and twenty children lined up with parents and other attendants before the font.

These vast numbers presented the minister with a problem in organisation – how to ensure that the child and the name would always exactly coincide. After various unsuccessful attempts at securing properly ordered lines he fell back upon a simple system whereby simultaneously with being handed the child for baptism he was to be handed by the father a slip of paper with the name or names clearly printed on it in block capitals. This proved effective and all went well for some months. One Sunday when he was progressing along the line he was handed a child, but there was no slip of paper. 'The name,' he whispered to the nervous father. 'Spindona,' the parent replied. 'I beg your pardon,' said the minister. 'Spindona,' repeated the father loud and clear, the mother nodding agreement from the side-lines.

It seemed a strange name, but if five years in a housing scheme had taught him nothing else it had convinced him that nothing is too strange to be true – and that people have strange ideas in the choice of names. So 'Spindona' was duly christened in that name.

In the vestry afterwards the father remarked, 'That was an awfu' braw name ye gi'ed the wean.' 'I thought it a bit unusual myself – is that not what she's called? 'Och no, we just cry her Jane.'

Further enquiry revealed that not only had the name Jane been written in block capitals on a slip of paper, but for added security the paper had been affixed to the child's christening robe with a pin. In the dialect of Glasgow 'It's pinned on her' can easily be the subject of considerable misunderstanding.

The problem is not how you get into that kind of mess but how you get out of it!

I like the tale of the dreamer who very much to his loss allowed reality to catch up with him just a moment too soon. It's a fair example of where good reasoning can take you when it is within a faulty framework.

'A terrible thing happened to me just before I got up this morning,' said the man to his mate. 'I dreamed I went to visit old Mrs M'Sporran and after we had been cracking for quite a while she said to me, 'I wonder would you care for a glass of whisky?'

'That's very kind of you Mrs M'Sporran,' I said – and I can hear myself saying it, 'but do you know I'm, awfully partial to toddy – do you think you could make it a toddy?' 'Of course,' says she, 'that would be no trouble at all. Just give me a minute till I put on the kettle for some hot water.' Away she went to the kitchen and, would you believe it, at that very instant the alarm went off and I woke up. If I hadna been so bloomin' fussy I could have had the whisky drunk.'

A great many of the jokes about the stupid Irishman in such wide circulation today are of the type 'too, too utterly ridiculous' even to begin to be funny. I do like the following, however.

Paddy went into the pub and asked for 'a lager and lime without any lime.' 'Now you got me beat there,' replied the publican, 'lime is a thing I don't have in the shop. How would it do, Paddy, if I was to give you the lager without any lemonade? That's a thing I got plenty of.'

I cannot imagine that the following incident ever occurred, but it would be nice to think that it did, the answer is so very neat. One trouble about it, of course, is that it is already 'dated' and the day is not far distant when changing television patterns will have rendered it quite meaningless.

A none-too-regular penitent had spent quite a bit of time in the confessional running through a few of the sins that were the present burden of his conscience – a not inconsiderable burden some might have thought. He had an odd sensation that things were not quite normal, there seemed a lack of response from the other side of the curtain. So he drew aside the curtain a little and peered through. He was horrified to see not the priest whom he expected but a woman busy with a feather duster.

'I am sorry,' he stammered, 'but I thought I was speaking to Father Mason.'

'No,' said the cleaner.' Father Mason's not here any more – he was transferred to Clydebank about six weeks ago.'

The penitent was still a bit confused. 'I didn't know there had been any changes,' he stuttered. 'You see I thought I was talking to Father Mason.'

'No,' persisted the woman, 'as I tell you, Father Mason is away and won't be back.' Then she added, 'In any case if one half of what you've been telling me in there is true it's not Father Mason you want to talk to about it – it's Perry Mason.'

The same considerations apply to this pre-marriage encounter in the vestry. You cannot but admire the wit of the minister portrayed and feel that he should have had a chance of exercising it in more promising circumstances.

The minister was in something of a dilemma. He had a couple in the vestry all lined up to be married. Both wore blouses and slacks, both had hair resting on their shoulders, both wore high-heeled platform shoes, both had varnished nails and had their fingers smothered in rings, both reeked of perfume, both had very effeminate features and bean-pole figures. Who was he to marry – and to whom?

He had a brainwave. 'I wonder,' he said, 'if before we go into the Church could I ask one of you to kiss the bride.'

It may be a long distance from the Church vestry to the race enclosure, but it's not so very far from the above story to the following one.

The punter observed that a priest was taking a great deal of interest in one of the starters. Indeed it looked as though he was subjecting it to a series of blessings.

Now the punter could not have been said to be a deeply religious man in the sense that he believed the entire creed of the Church, but he was a deeply religious man to the extent of believing that a horse carrying the official blessing of the Church started the race with a distinct advantage and one that counted for far more than a few pounds in the saddle. Such a horse must be expected to finish with an extensive lead. So he backed it heavily. When at long last the animal came ambling home a good way behind the rest of the field he felt not merely annoyed but positively cheated. Seeing the offending priest he approached him and told him what he thought of the quality of his blessing.

'You've got it all wrong, my friend,' said the man in holy orders, 'I wasn't blessin' the baist; I was givin' it the Last Rites.'

The business of picking a winner is not, it would seem, just an affair of the racecourse, as is illustrated by this ridiculous story about Making Ends Meet. They at least had a system, which is more than can always be said for debtors.

Every effort to recover the considerable sum due to them in settlement for goods delivered having failed to produce so much as an acknowledgment, the firm wrote the young man a most peremptory epistle of the type that begins:

'Unless' and ends 'within seven days from this date'.

This at least elicited a reply – almost by return. The letter, after deploring the very curt manner in which the firm had seen fit to address one of its esteemed customers, went on to say, 'Let me explain to you our method of book-keeping. All accounts are carefully filed away as they come in. Then each month immediately after I have paid my salary cheque into the bank my wife and I put all the outstanding accounts into a hat and we pull out and settle these to the extent of our credit. Those unpaid are laid aside to be given a further chance next month. And so on . . .'

'I should just like to make it clear that in the event of my receiving from you any further communication in the tone of your recent letter your account will not go into the hat.'

If all we are looking for is sheer unmitigated stupidity it would be hard to outdo the story of the patient who took his 'spare-tyre' to the doctor – it would have been difficult for him to go without it. 'Well Mr Jones,' said the doctor as he appeared in the surgery doorway, 'and what's the matter with you?' 'Well, doctor,' said the patient 'it's this that's worrying me,' patting with affectionate hands a much more than adequate paunch.

'Yes,' agreed the doctor, 'there's no doubt you've been putting on the weight. That's a great corporation you've got. I wonder you never thought to diet.'

'Oh doctor, it's no' the colour o' it that's worryin me – it's the size.'

There's something extraordinarily kindly and homely about the following, no matter how extravagant it may be.

The local councillor was visiting an elderly lady constituent in her council house. She wanted to make him a cup of tea and he gladly accepted the offer. He was horrified, however, to find just how much effort was involved for the old soul who, even with the aid of a stick, moved with difficulty. She had to make quite a few trips back and forth to the kitchen before the tea-tray was equipped to her complete satisfaction and when at length she arrived with the tea-pot she appeared quite exhausted.

As they were enjoying their cuppa the Councillor suggested that a hatch to connect the sitting-room to the kitchen would surely be a real help to her. She didn't seem too clear just what he was getting at, but she agreed that moving back and forth between the apartments was proving increasingly difficult. The councillor undertook to see the work put in hand.

On the occasion of his next visit he was happy to observe that the hatch had been duly installed. He was amazed, though, having accepted the usual offer of tea, to see that she hirpled back and forth exactly as before. 'I'm surprised,' he said, 'to see that you're not using the hatch.'

'Oh that,' she replied, 'it was real kind of you to put yourself to so much bother about it. But, you know, I'm getting that stiff I'm far quicker just going out through the hall than trying to squeeze through that thing.'

It would be hard to conceive of a situation more utterly incredible than that of the Highways Inspector who in highly incriminating circumstances was awaiting the arrival of an SMT bus. It's really a rather funny story and that is due once again to the basically sound line of argument that leads to the outrageously false situation.

Complaints had been received from the owner of a dwelling-house at the corner of a side street to the effect that the main road had been allowed to get into such a condition that his house was in danger of collapse, shaking ominously every time a vehicle passed. A Highways Inspector was sent to the house to investigate the complaint.

The lady of the house insisted that he come in and experience the vibration at first hand. A few cars having passed as he stood in different parts of the room the good man indicated that he hadn't noticed any particular vibration. 'Oh but,' said the hostess, 'you've no idea what it's like up the stair – come up to the bedroom and feel it for yourself.'

Standing at the bedroom window as a bus rattled past the Inspector conceded that he had felt a slight suggestion of a tremor but certainly nothing to indicate any degree of danger to the structure. But the lady was persistent. 'You want to feel it when one of these red SMT buses goes past, they're easily the worst. And,' she added, 'you want to be lying in bed at the time. Sometimes at night when I'm lying in that bed I actually think I'm going to be thrown out on to the floor when one of these red buses is passing. In fact,' she went on, 'there is one due any minute now. Just you lie down on the bed and feel it for yourself.'

Being an obliging kind of Highways Inspector he did as he was bidden and being a well-domesticated type he first removed his shoes and also for fear of crumpling the quilt he took the precaution of lying down underneath it.

Hardly was he settled down and before the bus had had the chance to arrive when the door was thrown open and the master of the household appeared in person in the bedroom. Seeing this unexpected visitor occupying his bed he not unnaturally asked what he thought he was doing there.

'I know you're not going to believe this,' said the somewhat embarrassed guest, 'but I'm just lying here waiting for an SMT bus.'

However incredible the foregoing story may be it at least relates an incident that lies within the realm of possibility in the sheer physical sense. Here, on the other hand, is a tale so completely divorced from reality that nobody could possibly try to pass it off as genuine. Yet for all its extravagant stupidity it exhibits its own brand of humour. Somebody will laugh at it.

The tenant had complained long, loud and bitterly that his house was infested with vermin, particularly with rats. After the complaint had been lodged many times authority got around to sending an inspector to look into the situation. 'Come into the room,' said the tenant, 'and you'll see the rats for yourself – we're tripping over them in here.' They stood for a few minutes in the room without any rats appearing. 'That's funny,' said the tenant, 'but just wait a minute while I lift this floorboard and then you'll see plenty.' Suiting the action to the words he lifted a floorboard. 'You watch there and you'll see them scurrying by.'

At the end of a few moments' vigil the inspector got off his knees. 'That's the queerest thing,' he said, 'I haven't seen a single rat. But I could have sworn I saw a fish swimming past.'

'Come on, now,' said the tenant, 'we'll take one thing at a time. You're here to see about the rats. We'll deal with the rising damp later.'

Again the logic of the following silly story seems impossible – even though the conclusion might well be generally acceptable. At least you can see the joke – with or without your bunnet.

The new recruit was proving extraordinarily raw, not to say incredibly stupid. Even the proposition that one and one make two seemed to elude him. After some pretty heavy spade-work he was got to agree that if he lost the sight of one eye he would be half-blind, whereas if he lost the sight of both he would be completely blind. Further he agreed that if someone were to cut off one of his ears he would be half-deaf. 'And what,' patiently asked the instructor, 'if both your ears were to be cut off?'

'I wouldna' be able to see at all,' came the unhesitating reply.

'Don't be stupid. What have your ears got to do with seeing? How do you make out that you would be totally blind if both your ears were to be cut off?'

'Well, can ye no' understand – my bunnet would fall down over my eyes.'

Talking of ears and eyes reminds me of a farmer whose hearing was getting a bit dicey. 'I'm no' hearin' very weel,' he confided to a friend. 'I manage no' too bad wi' this lug,' tugging at the left ear, 'but so far as the ither yin goes I canna hear a word. If it wasna for the look o' the thing I'd be every bit as weel wantin' it.'

The advantage of two ears from the point of view of the symmetry of the face is a consideration that might not immediately occur to everyone.

The same farmer was also responsible for what I have always thought of as a masterpiece of analogy. We were talking of a man who suffered from a very bad squint. 'He doesna' see very weel,' my friend explained, 'his e'en are no' hung true.' Better that one if you can.

To return to the case of sound logic within a framework of the most unlikely tale there is the following story, whose moral seems to be that one half of the world does not know how the other half bathes. Just as well, too.

> A firm of pottery manufacturers who specialised in bathroom furniture were reviewing their designs and to assist them in assessing what the public really wanted they had a number of representatives interviewing people here and there in random samples throughout the country.
>
> The representative covering Glasgow was greatly intrigued to come upon a man who claimed that he invariably sat in the bath with his back to the taps. No, he never sat any other way. Yes the other members of his family all did exactly the same. They had been doing so for the past five years. They would not dream of having a bath any other way.
>
> The man agreed that he was prepared – if all expenses were paid – to travel to London to discuss this unusual habit with the chief designer. That gentleman asked him questions of every sort but could do nothing to shake him in his devotion to what in nautical terms might be termed 'the blunt end o' the bath'.
>
> Something must surely have happened five years ago that led to this dramatic change in your habits, the blue-print man insisted.
>
> 'That's right,' the Glasgow man agreed, 'we lost the plug.'

A caricature may be so extravagant in its portrayal as quite literally to represent no man ever seen on sea or land and yet to be instantly identifiable not only as human but as a particular human being. One special feature had been blown up to an extent where it far exceeded the most extreme example nature had ever produced, but for all that the result was instantly recognisable because of the prominence on the original. It's a way of poking fun by sheer exaggeration.

The same kind of considerations can apply in the case of funny stories. The tale may be extravagant to the point where the alleged incident can be instantly repudiated and yet it is the kind of thing that is much in character. It may be used to focus attention upon some feature of life and through the medium of laughter make a criticism of it. I imagine Gulliver is the supreme example of what I'm talking about.

As an example I take the subject of the lay magistrate. The following, I am happy to believe, never occurred. And yet it makes a point which anyone with experience in this field will instantly corroborate.

The Baillie had taken his seat on the bench in the small town police-court and the first case was called. As the accused was brought in the magistrate recognised an old friend.

'Hallo, Sammie, what are you doing here?' he asked in tones of familiarity. 'I got nabbed last night for drunk and disorderly but I was nothin' o' the kind,' came the answer from the dock.

'Don't you try to come that story wi' me,' parried the bench. 'If you hadna been guilty you would never have got lifted. It's fellas like you that bring the name o' this town into disrepute. You'll go to prison for fourteen days.'

Meanwhile the Clerk of the Court was mildly protesting, 'Your honour, eh your honour, I think it might be better if we began by hearing the charge and then we could take a plea and hear the evidence.'

As a commentary upon one aspect of race relations I'm sure this little Pakistani tale from Glasgow belongs in the same category as the foregoing – it's a kind of caricature. I think it's worth telling although it's certainly incredible – not to be believed that men with so extensive a vocabulary should not have a better grasp of how the words ought to be used.

The three Pakistanis were discussing family matters. One was regretting that he had no children, this being due to the fact that his wife was unbearable.

One of the friends who had been longer in Glasgow hastened to correct the linguistic slip. 'You mean she is inconceivable,' he said.

The third member of the group, who was by way of being an authority on the language put them both right, 'What you try to say is that she is impregnable.'

This one is utterly and ridiculously impossible, but it does make a splendid story with a denouement which in my experience takes most people by surprise. At least for purposes of after-dinner speaking that is a great commendation of any joke. The one that you can see coming a mile away is the one to be avoided – that is, if you have a choice.

It was a bleak, cold, winter's night when the proverbial Englishman, Scotsman, Irishman and Welshman happened to bump into one another in The Strand. They were standing shivering as they commented upon the strange coincidence of their meeting, when their number was increased and the coincidence heightened by the arrival of their common friend, Isaac. After joining in the crack for a moment or two Isaac generously enquired, 'But vy do ve stand here and shiver in the rain? Vy do we not go into the hotel and 'ave a meal? So we could talk in comfort.' Suiting the action to the words he led the way into the nearby Savoy Hotel.

Needless to say the invitation was taken up with alacrity and a wonderful time was had by all. The most exotic dishes the menu had to offer, the most expensive vintages the wine-list had to suggest, the fattest cigars the waiter could produce – all were sampled with relish – a relish in no way diminished by the thought that someone else would be paying the bill. Replete at last the various members of the company felt much more mildly interested than personallly involved when they observed a waiter hovering in the background wondering upon whom to serve what was obviously the bill – not rendered a whit the more palatable because served on a silver salver.

The waiter's problem was resolved for him and considerable surprise was caused among the company when the Scotsman in a loud voice and a markedly Scots accent proclaimed, 'Here, waiter, gi'e me the bill. I insist. This nicht's party's on me. No, I wadna hear o' onybody else payin'. Leave this little affair for me to settle.'

Behaviour so completely out of character for a cannie Scot was enough not only to surprise the company but to earn a column in the next day's newspaper, where indeed it appeared on the front page. It was under a banner headline which read, 'Ugly Scene at the Savoy: Jewish Ventriloquist Murdered by Angry Scot.'

As a joke I think the following is a perfect parallel of the above and has the same power to take the hearer by surprise. The conclusion is so extreme as never to have been envisaged by even the most agile mind among your hearers.

The man visiting the pet shop was in search of a parrot.

'I'm very sorry, sir,' said the proprietor, 'but that's a bird I just do not have. You've no idea how difficult it is these days to get hold of a really good parrot. Now if I could interest you in a mynah bird. I have a couple of beauties here, both wonderful speakers – just listen to this . . .' His sales talk was broken into by the customer's insistence. 'I'm no wantin' a mynah bird. It's got to be a parrot or nothing.'

As I tell you, sir, they're practically unprocurable. But a budgie, now there's a lovely bird . . .'

Again he was rudely interrupted, 'Look, will ye no' listen when I tell you I want a parrot and a parrot it's got to be. I'll let you into the secret – I'll tell you why it's got to be a parrot. It's like this – I'm going to a fancy-dress ball next month and there's a competition for the best costume. The first prize is a Ford Escort and I'm bloomin' well goin' to win it. I'm dressin' up as Long John Silver. Noo would I no' look a richt stupid comin' hirplin' in on my crutch wi' a budgie on my finger.'

The shopman agreed that the overall effect would not be enhanced by a budgie understudying for the traditional parrot. 'I tell you what I'll do for you, sir. I buy most of my birds from a firm in Brussels – it's one of the best in Europe. If there's a parrot to be got anywhere they'll certainly get it for me. But it will take a day or two for the thing to be organised. Look, this is Monday. Suppose you come in a week on Wednesday and I'll see what I can do by then.'

'Right,' replied the pirate in embryo, 'a week on Wednesday it is.' Then he remembered. 'Oh no, I canna come in then – that's the day I've arranged to go into hospital to get the leg amputated.'

'I see your difficulty, sir,' said the salesman, 'there's no use doing a thing by halves.'

By and large I am not a devotee of the type of Irish joke in circulation today and which would qualify for inclusion here if stupidity were to be the test of eligibility. I would make an exception, though, in the case of the following because the stupidity here is so cleverly arranged.

Paddy had arrived in Glasgow straight from the Emerald Isle and he was hoping with the aid of some friends to secure some of that lucrative labouring employment in the building industry of which such rosy accounts had been filtering back home. One of his friends arranged an introduction to a site foreman, but nothing came of it. Paddy explained that he had been asked what he knew of this and that and when he confessed to complete ignorance the foreman's interest had evaporated, 'Ach now ye'll niver get yerself a jab if that's how ye're goin' to go about it. If ye're asked do you know how one of them machines works you tell them you know fine – once you get yourself a start the bhoys on the jab'll not see you stuck.'

An introduction to a different foreman was arranged. 'Do you know anything about working a mechanical digger?' Paddy was asked. 'A mechanical digger,' said he in derisory tones. 'I tell you what it is, I could take wan o' them things to bits wid me eyes shut an' wid my hands tied behind me back.'

The next question had to do with his familiarity with bulldozers. 'Do you know what I'm going for to tell you, the last jab was on I used to take them things to bits an' put them together again in the dark. There's nothin' you can taich me about bulldozers.' The foreman expressed satisfaction. 'We could do with a fellow like you,' he said, 'how about starting on Monday?' 'That would just suit grand,' said Mr Knowall. 'Right said the foreman, 'you'll report at the site at 8 o'clock. I'll tell you how you get there. Do you know Bishopbriggs?'

'Know Bishop Briggs? I knowed Bishop Briggs twenty years ago when he was a humble parish priest back home in Ireland.'

Maybe this other Irish story is not stupid enough to qualify, for it probably comes very near to the mark.

A farmer had his little place intersected by a railway line so that one field lay separated from the rest of his holding by a high embankment. To allow acess this was pierced by a cattle-creep. A railway linesman going about his business one day heard strange noises coming from below and went down to investigate. He found Paddy with a hammer and chisel laboriously cutting a couple of channels into the stonework of the roof of the creep. 'What in all the world is this you're up to?' he asked. 'Well you see, I've havin' a bit of trouble here,' said Paddy. 'I've got turnips in the field through there and I'm tryin to get them home to the farm. But it's the divil's own job gettin' Biddy my donkey through here, for she's rubbin' her ears on the roof. So I'm just takin' an inch or two out.'

The railway official was stupified. 'Paddy,' he said, 'did it never occur to you to take a spade and shovel two or three inches out of the floor?'

'Man,' replied Paddy, 'you don't rightly understand what I'm after tellin' you. It's not her feet that are catchin' – it's her ears.'

And when I'm in the way of Irish stories I must include this one which is very far from being stupid – or even, perchance from being a joke. Indeed it might well be thought to represent a shrewd comment upon a land where long memories and long knives seem to keep tragic company.

Bringing home his peats in panniers on the donkey's back Danny had occasion to ford a stream. One day the burn being in spate he forced the beast into the water where she missed her footing and was caught by the current and washed downstream. A week or two had passed ere he was back and by this time the water had reverted to its normal trickle. The ford was ankle deep in still water, but the donkey refused to cross. Not all his cursing and beating would make her budge an inch.

'You stupid baist, you,' he said in exasperation, 'yer memry's better nor yer judgment.'

It may be something in the atmosphere that causes it – I wouldn't know – but the assessment seems to apply to more than just the livestock.

Clearly it is to this department of humour that a whole chapter of tales belongs, under the general heading The Pearly Gates Group. Since all of these have to do with producing a picture of life after death they have in full measure the element of unreality and what makes them funny (when they happen to be funny and some of them emphatically are not) is the way in which the values of this world are carried over into the world to come. The element of eternity is cleverly used to enable judgment to be passed upon the things of time. That, some would say, is what Christian standards are all about, that is precisely the criterion that is employed – see things against the backdrop of eternity. But not quite in the same way as with the pearly-gates jokes!

If, for example, what you have in mind is a kindly crack at the ministry here is a tale you can tell.

The couple had been courting for many years without ever getting round to marriage, so that when they were involved in a fatal motor-crash and arrived outside the Pearly Gates in a state of single blessedness they felt they had put off rather too long. the first thing they did, therefore, was to explain their unhappy plight to Peter and to ask whether he could find them the services of a minister so that they might officially enter upon eternity in wedlock. It was with some disappointment that Peter finally returned to apologise that they didn't seem to have in such a thing as a minister.

It does seem rather a roundabout road to achieve a crack at the ministry. It may be course, that since the locus is heaven there is an added satisfaction to be got from, as it were, beating him on his own ground.

I do like the story of the 'Graduated Travel Scheme'.

The parish minister, having just died, had arrived in terms of the best tradition at the Pearly Gates. The person in charge at Check-point Peter explained that distances were considerable in the Land of Bliss and so transport was provided for all the inmates, but he would not be surprised to learn that in heaven things were arranged vastly differently from below. Here the quality of the transport was a perfect reflection of the driver's true worth, not just of the show he had been able to put on.

His informant went on to explain to him that he, the parish minister, had secured a very high rating, for although the world had failed to recognise his many admirable qualities and devotion to duty these things had not gone unobserved in higher places. When he went out to the street he would find a Jaguar awaiting him – with a full tank.

Sure enough, there was the car. Now our late lamented friend had never driven anything grander than a Mini and that at fourth hand – so he was proceeding very slowly, deliberately and nervously when out of a side-street and without warning there emerged a miserable jallopie which was unable to stop on the gold-paved street and crashed into his wing. It didn't occur to our friend – who was of a serious turn of mind – that spare parts were probably easily found in these heavenly regions and he was wondering where to turn.

To his utter amazement he saw emerging from the driving-seat of the other vehicle a figure whom he instantly recognised as the Archbishop of Canterbury, recently deceased. That dignitary came hurrying over, brimful of apologies, 'You know,' he said, 'this has just not been my day. Why it's not ten minutes ago that I knocked the Pope off his bicycle.'

It would be hard to conceive a story longer, more complicated, more remote-from-reality, more packed with contradictions than the foregoing. And less funny when at length the end of the tale has been reached. Against this there is something perfectly delightful, is there not, in the denouement of this final tale.

It was in the closing minutes of a hard-fought cup-final. They were already in extra time and it seemed certain the teams would by tie-ing at two goals each. Just as the referee was taking in a mouthful of wind to blow the final whistle the St Mirren centre-forward scored a remarkable goal to put his team ahead and give them the cup.

The player himself was very conscious of the fact that he had been off-side and that the goal should have been disallowed, but neither the referee nor the linesman had apparently noticed the fact, the goal had been awarded, the score was Celtic 2 St Mirren 3. The winning team went mad with joy, the terracing errupted with applause and the centre-forward was the hero of it all.

The centre-forward was an honest man – an unusually honest man – and he was miserable. As he was driving home after the match he was agonising over what he ought to have done. Should he have approached the referee and demanded that the goal be disallowed? Should he make some representations even now so that the whole affair could be looked into afresh? So deeply engrossed was he wrestling with his spiritual problem that he wasn't keeping a proper look-out, with the result that he got involved in a collision in which he was killed.

Arriving at the Pearly Gates, he found himself confronted by a saintly, bearded figure who enquired whether he had anything on his conscience to declare.

'Oh yes,' he said and he gave a resume of all that had happened in the closing minute of the game. 'What must I do?' he asked. 'There is absolutely nothing for you to do,' said his saintly interviewer, 'it was a perfectly good and proper goal – you've a lot to make you proud, nothing whatever to worry about.'

The player still insisted that he had definitely been off-side. 'Nothing of the kind,' said the saintly one. 'I was there myself and I saw the whole incident. It was a perfectly good goal – and achieved a well-earned win for your team.'

'But,' stuttered the player, considerably taken aback, 'I never thought, Saint Peter, that you would attend a football match.'

'My son,' replied the saintly one, 'I'm not Saint Peter, I'm Saint Mirren.'

CHAPTER THIRTEEN

UNDER THE INFLUENCE

'WELL YOU SEE, THERE WAS THIS DRUNK MAN . . .' I wonder how many funny stories have begun with those or similar words. Let us say the drunk man is always fair game for a laugh. Why so? Has it ever occurred to you as strange that although today (unhappily) drunkenness must be nearly as common among women as among men you find that the fair sex in their cups are held up to ridicule scarcely at all. It may well be that the sight of a woman under the influence moves us in a different kind of way; it may even be that the sight of a lady in that condition reveals to us in a way that will not be denied that this is not a subject for mirth but for pity and regret.

What is it anyway that is so mirth-provoking about the sight of a man under the influence? I imagine the answer may well be that with sufficient drink taken a man's defences are down, he is no longer capable of the sophisticated reaction to a situation that has become second nature to us all in conditions of sobriety and we find a measure of enjoyment in the degree of naivety that is the result. We see someone reacting in the honest way we ourselves would like to react but daren't. *In vino veritas* is a true enough statement, for in vino one loses the ability to conceal the truth in the rather clever way we all normally incline – and want – to do.

One of the interesting consequences of drinking is that a drunk man acquires a remarkable insensitivity to physical hurt – not only so, he appears to be protected against it. It's not just that he doesn't feel hurt; he isn't hurt. This is perhaps fortunate when one considers how susceptible such a man is to accident and misadventure. Clearly I remember on one occasion seeing a drunk man taking a tumble that for any sober citizen would at the least have involved an ambulance and a visit to a casualty ward, but this particular citizen, having apparently sufficient drink taken, picked himself up, dusted the knees of his trousers, and staggered upon his way. I am sure he was sore in the morning, but not at the time. A policeman in Greenock once remarked to me *à propos* a shipyard worker who had been knocked down by a car and whom I should have taken for dead, 'These fellows can stand a lot – especially with a bit of drink in them.'

In the same kind of way, I imagine, the drunk man is impervious to the jokes made about him, though you're wise not to laugh too heartily when he's around. I have heard the suggestion that a good cure for drunkenness would be if someone would take a few moving pictures and a tape-recording of a man in his cups and play it all back to him under conditions of sobriety. I am not satisfied it would be a cure, but I find it difficult to believe that the man himself would laugh too heartily at the sight and the sound of his own drunken antics.

I wonder, for instance, whether the hero of the following anecdote from my own experience had any recollection of his night's actvities, and how he would have reacted had he learnt exactly what he had been up to.

It was a cold December Saturday night – indeed it must have been been about two o'clock on the Sunday morning – when our Manse was thrown into noisy confusion by the barking of the dogs. Our Manse stood in its own grounds, well back from the road, with a long range of outbuildings separated from the back-door by an open court- yard. Our bedroom was a couple of floors up and we had at the time two dogs which slept and kept watch in the kitchen. An unusual noise in the road could be enough to disturb them and it could be quite difficult to get them to settle down again. There were times indeed when it was necessary to let them out to prowl around for a minute or two so to satisfy themselves that all was indeed well before they would settle.

On this particular occasion I had been in the first deep sleep of the night when the din started, so that I was still far from fully awake as I staggered down the stairs, yawning and dragging on a dressing-gown. The dogs refused to be comforted by either kindly words or threats, so I went to the back door to let them satisfy themselves there was nothing to be annoyed about. Imagine then my surprise on opening the door to find myself confronted by a stranger, a well-dressed man of middle age. 'Sh-shorry to dishturb you,' he said, 'but could you tell me how to get to the village?'

There are in fact two villages – Houston and Crosslee – and the Manse lies between the two so I naturally asked which village he wanted. 'Thash the damnable bit,' he replied, 'I cannot for the life of me remember the name of the village.'

Refraining from commenting on the fact that two o'clock in the morning seemed an odd hour to be seeking an unknown destination I contented myself with enquiring whether it was Houston. 'No, it's not Houston.' With equal confidence he assured me that it wasn't Crosslee. Could it have been Bridge of Weir? 'Thash it, Brish of Weir.' I explained that Bridge of Weir was two miles away and gave him directions. He thanked me very civilly, apologised again for the inconvenience and departed on a none-too-steady course.

I got the dogs settled down and went back upstairs, my teeth positively chattering with the cold. Needless to say, my wife was fully awake by this time and wanted a full eye-witness account of all that had been going on.

I seemed to have just fallen over again – it was in fact two hours later – when once more the dogs broke out into a fury of barking. Again I trudged down the stairs, again I swore at the dogs (without effect), again I threw open the back door, and again – believe it or not – I was confronted with the well-dressed middle-aged stranger. As I gasped for breath he happily explained, 'It's not Brish of Weir at all, it's Bishopton the name of the village I'm wanting. It'sh a funny thing, but for the life o' me I couldna' mind the name.' Carefully I gave him directions for the six-mile walk to this new destination, and the last I saw of him he was heading, happily if none too steadily, for the road.

One of the interesting features of the case is that drunk, as he certainly was, he had contrived to pass the house of the local bobbie on his way to and from Bridge of Weir. Maybe it was just because I had given him such good directions the first time he felt confidence in putting his additional business my way!

I've often wondered since whether he ever got to Bishopton, at at what hour he arrived there, and – not least important – what sort of welcome awaited him on his arrival. Of course, he may have discovered that it wasn't Bishopton (Langbank, who knows). But I don't think so. For I feel sure that if he discovered on arrival at Bishopton that that wasn't his destination he would have had the courtesy to come back and tell me!

I have had my share of nocturnal incidents arising from drink taken. One arose out of an article that appeared in the press regarding violence at football matches. In common with a number of other people I had been interviewed on the subject and the writer had quoted me quite extensively. It was just after three the following morning that the phone rang and the Voice asked me whether I was the person quoted in the *Daily Distress* on the subject of fitba' matches'. I pleaded guilty. 'Well you have said some things that I need to discuss with you.'

I indicated a willingness at a suitable time and place to discuss all he cared, but not on the phone at that hour. 'You mean,' he said, 'that you're not prepared to talk this over, man to man, with me just now?' I agreed he had got the situation perfectly.

'Well, let me tell you, I consider that a most ignorant attitude for you to adopt.'

I agreed he was probably right and hung up. But it was quite a while before I fell asleep for I was always expecting him to ring back. That he didn't do so must, I feel sure, have been due to his being without coppers and no-one being around to oblige him with change.

There are certain points of distinct similarity between these true stories and the classic tale – which I have always accepted as apocryphal – of the reveller who wanted to confer with the author of the Epistle to the Ephesians.

It was about four o'clock in the morning that a furious ringing of the doorbell at a house which on a large brass plate declared itself to be the residence of Dr Paul aroused that physician from his slumbers. Not wholly unaccustomed to emergency calls the worthy doctor hurried down the stairs. He was, however, not much

187

impressed to discover a gentleman whose dress showed that he had been having a night on the town, and whose general deportment indicated that it had been a reasonably successful one.

'Well, what is it?' he summarily enquired. 'Are you Paul?' asked the caller. 'Yes, I'm Paul.' 'Well, you know I've always wanted to meet you – if only for the sake of telling you I think yon was an awfu' guid letter you sent to the Ephesians.'

Dr Paul was not impressed and slammed the door. A few moments later the bell-pulling was renewed with redoubled vigour. It was by this time a furiously angry Dr Paul that opened the door, but before he could threaten his visitor with the police the latter said, 'You shouldn't have shut the door like that. I wasn't finished. I've always wanted to ask you, did you ever get a reply to yon awfu' guid letter you sent to the Ephesians?'

And I must confess to a fondness for the utter finality of the punch-line in this other story of midnight bell-pulling and nocturnal visitation. It would be nice to be able to do that kind of thing in response to some invitations, but sobriety and propriety can have such a restricting influence.

Arrangements were complete for an expedition that was shortly to set off on a voyage of exploration to the South Pole when at the last moment the photographer of the party took ill and had to call off. Through the media an SOS went out for a volunteer, application to be made to the leader of the expedition at an address in London's West End.

A couple of days later the leader was awakened at an outrageous hour of the morning by a furious din at his front door. Opening his bedroom window he demanded to know what was afoot.

'Is it you that's wantin' a photographer to go on an expedition to the South Pole?' enquired a swaying figure on the doorstep.

'Indeed it is,' replied the leader, 'just hold on a minute till I come down and we can talk things over.'

'Not at all,' said the voice, 'don't you bother to come down. I was just passing and I thought I should give you a knock to let you know that I'm one photographer that'll not be volunteering.'

There's something very satisfying too in the old tale of the two drunk men who had got into a furious argument as to whether the circular orb of light above them was the moon or the town-hall clock and who decided to submit the issue to arbitration but were unfortunate enough to choose as arbiter one who declared himself 'a stranger to the district.'

Its funny, isn't it, how when we are wanting directions we invariably pick on a stranger! Drunk or sober!

A very effective story used to be told by the late Sir James Miller (Lord Provost of Edinburgh and Lord Mayor of London). As nearly as I can I'll tell it as he did.

> I was travelling home to Edinburgh on a sleeper from King's Cross. Having got my things in my berth in good time I was enjoying a stroll on the platform and was amused to watch three men who had been about to board the earlier train on the other side of the platform looking carefully at the clock and then looking longingly at a notice which said Refreshments. Turning their back on the train they headed hurriedly in the direction of the notice. I was watching for their return and thought they must have decided to let the train go. But no. Just as the guard was about to flag the train away they came hurrying down the ramp. As they reached the platform one of them fell flat on his face, but the guard grabbed the other two and flung them into a compartment just as the train was moving off.
>
> I went over and helped the fallen one to his feet. I thought he might have been swearing, but to my surprise he burst out laughing. 'That's a right good laugh,' he said. I suggested there was nothing very funny about missing your train. 'Thash all right,' he said, 'I can get the next train. But these two that are away first stop Waverley, these two are my pals and they just came to the station to see me off.'

While, as I have suggested, the drunk man is encased in armour protecting him from embarrassment as a result of his activities the same does not apply to those with whom he comes into contact and who may be very vulnerable indeed. There could, for instance, be just enough point in the punch-line of the following tale to make it a bit awkward for the recipient and certainly enough to raise a hearty laugh at his expense.

It was with no little difficulty that the young soldier boarded the bus. The amount of equipment with which he was borne down would have provided an obstacle to the most sober of travellers, and our warrior most emphatically did not measure up to that description. Clearly he was returning to duty after a period of leave, and equally clearly the farewells had been conducted in the best spirit – and no want of it.

To make matters worse the bus was crowded and there wasn't a single seat available. There was plenty of room in the gangway and he was being mercilessly flung from one end of it to the other. A minister took pity on him. 'Look, my son,' he said, 'you're obviously in difficulty; you'd better have my seat.'

'Thank you, meenister, thank you very much indeed,' said the man of war happily relaxing into the seat. 'You know what I'm gonna tell you – you're the only man on this bus that kens what it feels like to be fu'.'

By and large, I do not find the standard drunk-man joke all that funny. At the same time a great many stories have accumulated around the subject of drink and drinking, and many of them I find highly entertaining.

There's the story they used to tell in Paisley about the weaver whose interest in theology deepened with his intake.

It was a Saturday evening in Paisley many years ago. Dr Gentles, who then was Minister at the Abbey, was wending his way along the High Street when he was approached on unsteady feet by one of his rather less than enthusiastic members, a weaver in the town.

Ere Dr Gentles could take evasive action John caught sight of his minister and made straight for him. 'Dr Shentles,' he began, 'Dr Shentles, there's a question I've been wanting to ask you. I want you to explain to me the doctrine of original sin.'

Having made a rough mental calculation of John's probable blood content the good Doctor replied, 'John, if you will come to see me some day when you are sober I shall be more than happy to explain to you the doctrine of original sin.'

'But, Minister, thash juist the trouble,' said the budding theologian, 'when I'm sober I don't give a tinker's curse for the the doctrine of original sin.'

It is apparently not exclusively an interest in theology that is in danger of evaporating with the clearing of the head. It can apply in the field of matrimony as well, as the following story illustrates rather convincingly.

The couple had come by arrangement to the Manse for a very quiet wedding. The Minister appeared all ready to conduct the ceremony. But one look at the bridegroom raised considerable difficulties in his mind. It was clear that the husband-to-be had contrived to anticipate a fair amount of the rejoicing that normally follows the wedding service.

The minister took him aside and asked him some questions from which it was apparent that he was in no fit state to commit himself to solemn vows that would be of life-long application. In these circumstances the Minister saw himself as having no alternative but to delay the whole affair. This he explained as gently as he could to the bride who burst into a flood of tears.

'Don't take it so badly,' said the Minister, 'it's only a matter of delay for an hour or two, or for a day at the most.

'As soon as he is sober you can get in touch with me and the pair of you can come along and we'll get on with it.'

'But that's just the trouble, Minister,' said the frustrated bride, 'You've no idea the job I've had getting him drunk enough to come. When he's sober he wants to stay single.'

Which reminds me of the tale of the bridegroom who was so nervous his vocal chords were affected to the extent that he couldn't say 'I do' – the best he could manage was a kind of stuttering 'I'd'. 'Och, Minister,' said the bride, 'you could surely make do wi' that – I'll make him say 'oo' all right when I get him home.'

Or, of course, there was the chap at the Anglican service so nervous (or inebriated) that when asked, 'Wilt thou take . . .' he replied, 'I wilt.'

But to return to our tales about inspiring bold John Barleycorn as Burns had it I think the following is a perfect gem.

The train was due to stand for a while at the junction. A gentleman leaned out of the window of a first-class compartment and enquired of a passing porter, 'Any chance of obtaining some liquid refreshment here?'

'I'm very sorry, sir,' replied the man in uniform in suitably lugubrious tones, 'nothing but tea or coffee.'

You can so easily picture the complexion of the man leaning out of the window – the kind of which they say in the country, 'It wasna soor milk pented yon' – and you can equally readily follow the reasoning of the porter. This is of the essence of a good joke – that so much does not need to be told, it tells itself. To be able to present so compelling a picture in fifty words is surely no small achievement.

I cannot vouch for the truth of the following, though I'm sure there was a time when it could have been possible.

Going along the village street one evening the Minister was appalled and saddened to come upon one of his elders 'taking the breadth of the road.' Approaching the inebriated one the Minister offered to take him home. 'Na, na,' said the elder, 'thank ye for the kind thocht, but I canna go hame for a while yet. I've still some cairds to gi'e oot.'

'Cards to deliver,' said the shocked divine, 'you don't mean to tell me that you are out in this condition delivering communion cards.'

Willie agreed that indeed this was so, and that, in fact, it was the hospitality that was forced upon him in the various homes that was responsible for his condition. It was not that he was all that fond of the stuff, but sheer politeness prevented you from saying No when it was actually thrust upon you. After all he had already made four calls this evening.

'But surely, you don't get drink given you in every house in your district.'

'No, that's right,' conceded William, 'I've got three teetotal households in my street. But I just shove their cairds through their letter-box.'

The records of my own old parish contain a rather pathetic narrative of a school-master prosecuted by the Kirk Session for drunkenness. It appeared that after the death of his wife he had taken to the bottle and had become what must surely be the most to be pitied of all inebriates, the solitary drinker. He shut himself in the schoolhouse for days on end and people could only jalouse what was going on. This they did very freely. This element of privacy, however, made extremely difficult the task of the Kirk Session in securing a conviction. Where to find evidence when he was never to be seen the worse for the wear.

But in the end a witness did come forward – none other than the widow who was the proprietrix of the public house whose garden abutted on that of the dominie. She testified that she had taken her two children away from the school because the master was in no fit state to teach them properly. But how did she know of this? Because she sold him the stuff over the garden wall, and no man could consume all that and be a good schoolmaster at the same time.

If moral principles come into conflict with business practices there can be little doubt which will survive.

While we are moving within the realm of kirk affairs it may be appropriate to tell this little tale with its ecclesiastical background – there's something distinctly fetching in the picture of the young man getting to see things really big, although for my own part the element of stupidity and incredibility far outweighs any real humour.

The young priest, it was reported, was not doing at all well in his new parish. His bishop went along one Sunday to discover, if he could, exactly what was amiss. He found that the young man – whom he knew to have considerable ability – became a bundle of nerves the moment he stood up in front of the congregation, with the result that he stuttered and stumbled and faltered and generally put up a most unconvincing show.

The bishop saw him afterwards, exhorting him to pull himself together. The young man explained that he always felt grand until he actually found himself face to face with the people. The bishop advised 'Just the merest sensation of a drop of gin immediately before the service to put a bit of fire into your preaching.'

The superior was considerably gratified when reports began to reach him of how things were picking up in the parish. Everyone was delighted with the young chap, the men folk in particular were turning out as they had never been known to do before. So he slipped in one Sunday and took a seat at the back. It was even as had been reported.

Once again he went round to see the young man afterwards – this time to congratulate him. 'But, if you will excuse my saying so, there were three places where you went wrong. First there are ten commandments, not a dozen as you so confidently affirmed. Secondly our blessed Lord had twelve disciples – I don't know where you got the idea there were a score. Thirdly the scripture tells us that David slew Goliath with a pebble and not – and here I quote your own words – not with a bloody great brick.'

Drink has, of course, the effect of making us feel really big and filling us with Dutch courage. This is not necessarily a good thing – it may be merely making us unaware of the real difficulties and dangers that lie ahead. Sometimes too, the advantage is offset by the fact that the difficulties and dangers are enlarged every bit as much as our strength is enlarged. You know, perhaps, of the cricketer who, as he left the pavilion for the crease was warned that he would see three balls coming towards him and that he must aim for the centre one. Returning clean bowled with the first delivery he explained that he had hit the middle ball all right but unfortunately had hit it with one of the outside bats.

Yes, alcohol can enable us to see things very big – if not always very clear – and there are drunk-man stories that are considerably larger than life. Like this one about the size of a penguin.

'On your way, gentlemen,' said the publican as two men staggered into the roadside hostelry, 'you're getting nothing to drink here. You've already had more than's good for you. So on your way.'

'Thash right,' agreed one of the visitors, 'thash perfectly right. But we're not wanting anything to drink. We were just wondering – my friend, my very good friend, and I – we were just wondering my very good friend and I whether you would be so good as to settle a small argument that has arisen between us and on which we have laid a little bet – just a very little bet.'

The publican indicated that if the matter was one within his competence he would be prepared to act as judge. 'What,' he asked, 'is the nature of the dispute that has arisen?' 'What size would you say, mister, is a penguin?'

'I would say they stand about so-high,' indicating a point about fifteen inches above floor level. 'O come on,' said the questioner, 'surely you'll get penguins an awful lot bigger than that.'

'I suppose you could. I expect they vary a bit. I imagine you could get them as high as that –' elevating the imaginary spot by four to six inches.

'But there must be penguins an awful lot bigger than that.'

'I believe there is a variety called a King Penguin. One of them might stand as high, say, as the counter.'

'Nothing higher than that – you're sure?'

'Absolutely certain.'

Turning to his partner who, up to this point had taken no part in the discussion, the defeated one handed over a five-pound note. 'Here's your money, Willie, you win. You must have been right enough when you said yon were two nuns we knocked down yon last village we passed through.'

Considerably more preposterous but none the less quite funny in its own ridiculous fashion is the tale of the chimpanzee chucker-out.

The publican had established a very successful business just off the motorway. Trade was brisk and he had built up an excellent clientele. His one worry was that on the odd occasion an undesirable would find his way in from the motorway and cause annoyance. It was outrageously expensive to maintain a chucker-out not needed for weeks on end. He learned that it was possible to obtain a chimpanzee specially trained for this kind of work. When not required for its specialised skills it would sit in a corner, disturbing no-one, but if trouble broke out its mere appearance in answer to a call was enough to daunt the bravest spirit and to restore order.

That is until the night when the wee Glasgow bauchle arrived on the scene. Where exactly he came from was never very clear. He just suddenly presented himself at the bar, clearly already very much under the influence, and demanded 'a double Scotch.' 'My friend,' said the publican, 'you've had as much as is good for you already. If you take my advice you'll . . .' 'I'm no' askin' for your advice, I'm askin' for a double Scotch. An' what's more ye'd better hurry up, for I havena' a' nicht to wait for it,' interrupted five-foot-three of Glasgow belligerence.

The publican repeated that his customer had already had enough and that he was getting no drink here. The little man proceeded to paint a thumb-nail sketch of what the premises would look like if he didn't get his double Scotch 'in two minutes flat'.

Obviously a case for zoological reinforcements – they had dealt effectively with this kind of attitude before. So the chimp having been whistled into action linked arms with the little man and led him quietly through the door. Noise of an intensity of quite a few decibels percolated through from outside. Then the little man reappeared carefully picking hairs from his jacket and trousers.

'Come on,' he said, 'hurry up wi' that double Scotch – I'm needin' it worse than ever noo. D'ye ken what I'm gonna tell ye. Thae Pakistanis – put wan o' them in a fur coat an' there's nae livin' in the same hoose wi' him.'

It would be quite unthinkable to have a chapter about drink and drinking without some reference to the north-west of Scotland where drinking is neither a relaxation nor a recreation but is just part of a way of life, and where, by and large, its effects have been so tragic. Perhaps, this little story will suffice, for in a way it illustrates rather neatly how important is a dram – especially a free dram.

A gentleman from London was spending a fortnight in a West Highland hotel enjoying the fishing. One of the hotel staff acted as his ghillie, rowing for him each day on the loch. Donald made no secret of the fact that he was greatly impressed with the deer-stalker which the gentleman from the metropolis affected as headgear. It had flaps which came down over the ears and Donald was sure it must be a great comfort to wear. He wondered whether he might be able to get such a thing to buy in Inverness, but on second thoughts he decided 'they would be much too dear for the likes o' me.'

When his holiday was over and he was preparing for the journey south the gentleman made Donald a present of his deer-stalker – he didn't know whether they would have that particular type in Inverness and he could easily get himself another in London.

Donald was as intensely grateful as anyone in the West Highlands can be expected to be. The following summer when he returned to resume his fishing the gentleman was surprised to notice that Donald was still in his accustomed bonnet. One day he ventured to ask what had happened to the deer-stalker. 'O but it was a wonderful hat,it was so comfortable, and it kept my head so luffly and warm. Do you know, from the day you gave it to me until the day of the accident it was never off my head.' 'The accident? I didn't know you had been involved in an accident, Donald. Whatever happened?'

'It was like this. I was out rowing on the loch with an American gentleman. It was bitterly cold and I was wearing my new hat, and very glad of it I was. It would seem that the gentleman asked me if I would care for a dram, and with these damn things over my ears I never so much as heard him. So I haven't been wearing it much since. But it is certainly a very fine hat – if you are out on your own.'

Talking of drinking as a way of life, one must not imagine that this has been confined to any one district or to any one class of society. In the West Highlands, however, it is a non-selfconscious affair in a way that is not universally so. As the following tale would seem to indicate there are those who are deliberate in their drinking and who in fact take pride in it. And that too can produce its amusing incidents.

The laird was inordinately proud of his well-earned reputation as a hard drinker. There was not a single member of the gentry for miles around that he had not had the satisfaction of leaving under the table after a session with the bottle.

Having got a new tenant-farmer on the estate he was interested to learn that this gentleman had himself established a reasonable record in feats of a like description among the farming community. A test of strength seemed called for. The laird invited the farmer to 'the big house' to discuss some point of agricultural policy. 'You'll have a dram, John,' he welcomed him. 'Man, laird, I wadna say No,' responded John in the tones of one who felt his position as a guest laid obligations of courtesy upon him.

The laird stretched for the bell-pull, and when the butler appeared said, 'Watkins, fetch us a bottle of whisky and two glasses.' From time to time as the evening advanced the butler was recalled – 'Watkins fetch me another bottle of whisky.'   Until one time on answering the bell Watkins entered the study to find his master neatly curled up on the hearth-rug. This time it was the farmer who gave the order: 'Watkins, fetch me anither laird.'

Are you able always to identify a drunk man? Hearken to this simple tale.

The odds seemed to be in favour of the view that the young man was sober, though it was no less evident that he had taken drink and not a little of it at that. He explained to the young lady who shared the seat with him that he was on his way into town to meet his wife and that she would be raging at him for being drunk when in fact he was nothing of the kind. It was his considered opinion, he made it clear, that the world was an unfair, unkind and ungenerous place. Anxious to be helpful his travelling companon suggested 'I'll tell you, Jimmie, exactly what you ought to do. Just where you get off the bus there's a fruit-shop. You slip in there and buy a bunch of flowers for Jenny, and I'm sure that when she sees you with them she'll be so charmed she'll not say a word about the smell of your breath.'

'Goad, Miss Broon,' said the horrified Jamie, 'if Jenny saw me comin' up the road wi' a bunch o' flooers in my hand she wad ken for certain I was foo.'

Let me finish the chapter with this yarn from Ireland, which, although it is not a drunk-man story, has to do with a man who had been drinking, and somehow you can still smell the liquor around.

The Irish priest was walking along a country lane in his parish on a fine spring morning when he came upon one of his less reputable members gathering himself out of the ditch, where it was obvious he had spent the night. 'A very good mornin' to you, Father,' said Patrick as he fell into step, adding ruminatively a few moments later, 'it's a terrible thing this sciatica, Father, a terrible affliction.'

The priest saw in this observation a not to be missed opportunity for driving home a moral lesson. 'I'll tell you, Patrick, exactly what sciatica is. Sciatica's nothing else but a judgment of

God, and it's visited upon them that deserve it.' Patrick was clearly shaken by this information.

Pressing home his advantage the priest went on to describe how one acquired sciatica, producing a formidable list including things like getting blind drunk and rolling about the roads at night, sleeping in ditches, flirting with other men's wives in lofts and behind hedges, and so on. Patrick was obviously distressed. 'That's a terrible story ye be after tellin' me, Father. It sure do set you thinkin'.'

Feeling that perhaps he had said enough to establish his point and that the time had come for a word of comfort, the priest enquired where exactly the pains were gripping him.

'Glory be to God,' replied Patrick, 'I don't have it at all. But I'm just done readin' in the paper that the bishop's got it awful bad.'

CHAPTER FOURTEEN

BIG DEAL

FOR THE BENEFIT OF ANY so benighted as not to be aware of the fact, the Tallies refers to the premises of the person of Italian descent who deals in ice-cream and other cognate products. With that word of explanation I pass to my story.

> The small Glasgow urchin presented himself at the counter in the Tallies, and demanded a bottle of Kola. The Tallie laid a bottle of the desired fluid on the counter.
>
> Having lifted and inspected it with some care the boy laid it back on the counter and enquired, 'Can I swap it for a limonade?' Without a word the shopkeeper put the Kola back in its place on the shelf, laying a bottle of lemonade on the counter in its stead. This the boy lifted and turned towards the door.
>
> 'Here,' said the Tallie, 'you havena paid me for that.'
>
> 'Naw,' freely admitted the budding man of affairs, 'I gi'ed you the Kola in exchange for it.'
>
> 'But,' persisted the Tallie, 'you never paid me for the Kola.'
>
> 'Of course I didnae,' said the boy: 'I never drunk it.'

I have always thought of that story as a peculiarly neat example of a sharp business transaction – so sharp that someone is bound to get cut. Everyone is prepared to laugh at that story because, I expect, no-one is prepared to take it seriously. And, presumably, what is not to be taken seriously is to be taken humorously. The business aspect of the affair apart, there is always something entertaining about an argument that sounds convincing but that you know is faulty even though you cannot put your finger with precision on what it is that renders it invalid. In this instance why should you be expected to pay for goods you have not consumed – indeed have returned to the seller untouched?

Sometimes in moments of cynicism – and these should, I am aware, be avoided at all costs – I have suggested that a transaction like the above when practised by the city gamin at the level where coppers are at stake will earn him a kick in the pants, but if carried through by the business tycoon on a plane where millions are involved will merit a mention in the Birthday Honours List. This, though, probably springs from a sour-grapes reaction on the part of one who has never been able to think up, let alone to carry through, anything half so clever. At least we'll attribute it to that – any attempt to take it more seriously could well land me in real trouble.

It's difficult to see why a story about a smart transaction should *ipso facto* be found amusing. That we should be filled with horror to think that anyone would be so dishonest, or that we should be filled with admiration to think that anyone should be so clever – these would be natural reactions. What is there about it that is so funny?

I am inclined to think it runs back into the doctrine I have mentioned elsewhere that the funny-ha-ha and the funny-peculiar are not really so far removed from one another as we are inclined to think, that in fact our gut-reaction to the unprecedented and the strange is to laugh – by way of self-defence. As animals will physically attack the stranger in their midst so we attack, with derisive laughter, that which does not fit into our philosophy, does not conform to our accepted pattern. For instance, the Jewish businessman, though he has been an accepted member of Scottish society for many generations, is still very much a stranger in our midst and we are ready to laugh at attitudes which to him are perfectly natural, because they are so utterly foreign to our normal habits of thought. The reaction to a proposed business deal and the considerations which make it worthwhile may be to us so outlandish as to provide us with a subject of mirth. Unable to comprehend it completely we laugh at it.

The following story about a 'deal' is so magnificent as to merit serious consideration long after we've finished smiling at its humorous aspect.

Isaac was offering to sell his friend Asher an elephant at the throw-away price of £500 – 'I do not sell it, I give it away to you for that,' he protested. 'Don't be stupid, Isaac, vot vould I vant with an elephant?' 'But,' insisted Isaac, 'it is the cleverest elephant you ever saw, young, healthy and strong. Tell you what I'll do. For you – but only because we have been such good friends for so long – for you I make it £450.'

'How often do I have to tell you I do not want an elephant. I have nowhere to keep an elephant. I do not want to be eaten out of house and home. I haff no use I can make of an elephant. Go away and have a ride on your elephant.'

'Look, Asher. Our fathers were friends years ago in Poland. Your mother was a good woman who did so many kindnesses. For old times' sake I bring down my price to £420. Just think before you say No again – £420 for a good strong Indian elephant.'

'I do not care suppose it is a Chinese elephant, I do not want it. For me it is just a white elephant. I tell you I have no place to keep it suppose you give it to me as a present.'

'I tell you what I'll do. I make it a package deal. I sell you three elephants, all for the price of £1200.

'Ah,' replied Asher, 'now you talk business. Now we do a deal I buy your three elephants for £1100. No.'

I think we do not normally recognise how deep the differences are between the attitudes to a business proposition adopted by the Jew and the Gentile respectively. Bernard Shaw in one of of his Introductions makes the point very forcibly in respect of one particular piece of business – a loan of money.

The Jew, Shaw claims, seeks a loan because he is temporarily embarrassed for want of cash in hand. When he does so he knows when and how he is going to be in a position to repay; and he is prepared to pay interest charges in respect of the service he has obtained. He finds it natural, too, to regard as a friend the person who is prepared to transact this business with him.

The Gentile, on the other hand, seeks a loan because he is in financial difficulties; he hasn't a clue when, how – or even whether – he will be in a position to repay; he resents the interest charge as 'usury', and he looks upon the lender as a blood-sucker. It can certainly be said among Gentiles that the surest way to lose a man's friendship is to lend him money. Even after the debt is fully paid – if it ever is – there can continue an attitude of resentment, for there's something not quite quite in having been in the position where you needed a loan, and the lender is an ongoing reminder of the borrower's shame.

Incidentally, you know about the chap who, when asked, 'Can you lend me £20?' said, 'No, but thanks for the compliment.'

There is something essentially amusing – as well as desperately sad – in the following true tale.

A small shopkeeper in the village had advanced one of his women customers £10 in answer to a heart-rending plea accompanied by a solemn promise to repay in a fortnight. The weeks passed but there was no sign of the slightest attempt to clean the slate.

The lender suggested to the lady that there seemed little likelihood of her having all that money to hand at the one time, so he would be prepared to take it at the rate of fifty pence a week and she could settle it each Saturday when she was in for her shopping. This was agreed to and, with the odd break for a week or two at a time this was what she did.

Just over two years after the loan had been given the final instalment was repaid. There was, of course, no suggestion of interest. Leaving the shop after paying her last fifty pence the woman ran into a friend of mine.

'He's a right mean one, that,' she said referring to her benefactor. 'Do you know this? I've just paid him back the last instalment of £10 that he lent me, and the best he had to say was 'Thank you'!

Clearly the least of what was to have been expected was that he would have given her back her last payment in recognition of her magnificent achievement in clearing the debt. A deep difference of attitude indeed.

Sometimes there's more than just a difference of attitude attributed to the Jewish man of affairs – the most outrageous suggestions are sometimes made in regard to his integrity. For example the tale of the businessman who wanted to know how to start an earthquake – he thought the insurance company might be suspicious if he had yet another fire.

A much more delicate allusion to methods sometimes resorted to when all else fails is contained in the following.

> Two Glasgow men met on the street. Said the one, 'I was terribly sorry, Abie, to hear of that frightful fire you had at your factory last Thursday.'
>
> 'Wheesht,' said his friend, 'it's next Thursday.'

One of what I consider the cleverest of all the stories I know in this class is a home product. Perhaps this should not be too much of a surprise, for it comes from Aberdeen where, it used to be said, a Jew could not make a living. It measures up very neatly to the title, 'Flogging a Dead Horse'.

> It was on a market day in Aberdeen that a local farmer ran into one of his neighbours. 'Hullo, Willie,' he greeted him, 'it's no' that often we see you in aboot the market. What's brocht you in the day?' 'Ach man, I had a bit o' business. I decided I was gaun to sell that auld grey mare o' mine,' Willam explained. 'Are ye sellin' her at last?' his neighbour replied. 'Man, ye didna need to bring her intae the market for that – I'm sure I've offered to buy her ofen enough. I'll gi'e ye a hunner pounds for her.' 'Done,' said his friend. They struck hands. The money was handed over. William describd where the mare was stabled. Buyer and seller parted company.
>
> A couple of drams later William began to feel sentimental about the old mare that had served him so faithfully for so long and decided that the least he could do was to visit the stable and take fond and formal farewell of her. On arrival at the stable he was shattered to find the mare lying dead – the excitement of a trip to town, it seemed, had proved too much for her aged heart.
>
> William now found himself confronted with a rather delicate problem. He had no real doubt in his own mind that the animal must have departed this life after rather than before she had become the property of his neighbour, but lest this view might not be shared – which seemed a very real possibility – he was unwilling to meet that gentleman until the first pangs of the latter's grief should have had time to subside a little.

The day advanced and as the evening approached William was thinking of setting off for home when to his horror he saw his neighbour drawing near. Instead, however, of the angry encounter for which he was prepared he saw his friend hurrying forward with hand outstretched, 'Man, Wullie, ye did me a richt guid turn this day,' he he said expansively.

'What kind o' guid turn?' enquired the more than surprised benefactor. 'Weel, ye mind how ye selt me yer auld mare for a hunner pound. Ye'll hardly believe me, but when I got to the stable to look at her she was lyin' there stone dead. I was wonderin' what to dae when I had a brain-wave. So I've been gaun aboot a' day tellin' folk I had an auld mare to sell but had decided she was hardly worth puttin' thro' the ring an' I was juist goin' to raffle her at £5 a ticket. D'ye ken I've selt near a hunner and fifty tickets. Aboot an hour ago we held the draw in the pub at the Bull's Head an' Jock Broon frae Back o' Hill won her. Of course when the pair of us got to the stable for me to hand her ower there she was lyin' dead.'

'What did ye dae then?'

'What could I dae? I gi'ed Tammie back his five pound, of coorse. I tell ye, Wullie, ye've done me a richt guid turn this day.'

The story is not, perhaps, as far-fetched as might appear. At least it must be agreed that the appeal of the raffle is almost irresistible – particularly among the hardest-headed of our citizens. I remember at a cattle-show seeing a bunch of farmers buying ticket after ticket for a wheel-of-fortune where the prizes seemed mainly to be things like silk tights. Admittedly the affair was in aid of some charity. But just try approaching one of these gentlemen with a straight appeal for a donation for that charity!

It is said – without foundation I'm sure – that in a certain kirk there had been a massive improvement in attendance at the evening service. The minister was asked by one of his colleagues how this had been done, had he made some significant change in the order of service? The service was as it had always been but for one small change, the minister said – where they usually had the sermon they now instead raffled the collection. It might be worth trying.

I stay with the kirk for my next example – not so much of big business as of slick business.

A certain beadle had been seen, it was believed, with his fingers in the plate to the extent that he had extracted a fifty-pence piece before carrying the offering from the front door to the vestry. A watch was set for the following Sunday and this time it was clear beyond all doubt that a fifty-pence piece had been taken and that he alone had opportunity. Bad news, for he was a good, obliging and reliable beadle and his honesty had been thought beyond question. But clearly he had to go.

The minister sorrowfully told him of the discovery and of the decision of the Kirk Session. Had he anything to say by way of mitigation? 'All I've got to say,' said John, 'is that if I hadna hanselled the plate ilka Sunday wi' that coin for the past six months your collections would not have been half as guid as they were.'

I remember one day talking to a young farmer in my parish and getting round to discussing a family that had recently moved into the district. They were people of great importance, wealth and distinction – or so at least they had assured us and so their standard of living seemed to indicate. The day before our conversation they had departed as suddenly as they had come, but they had neglected to leave a forwarding address, and this was found to be unfortunate by the many local tradespeople who had outstanding accounts to be posted on. This led to a more general discussion about 'chancers', their methods and the degree of success that so often seems to attend their efforts.

'They tell me, Mr Herron,' said my young friend. At this I pricked up my ears, for when Sandy resorted to this motif it was invariably as a lead-in to some gem of his own concocting. 'They tell me, Mr Herron, you should never steal anything in this world, ye're faur better to buy it an' no' to pay for it.'

There, if you will, is a whole philosophy of life, condensed into very small bulk. It contrives to say in a sentence as much as most of us could do in a paragraph – and more than some could do in a chapter. There, as I see it, is true Scots humour, unblemished by the faintest ripple of a smile.

It brings to mind another example of Scots humour (in the same field of high finance), an example characterised by the same dead-pan solemnity.

The parish minister was walking along the village street one Friday about tea-time when suddenly the peace of the whole neighbourhood was shattered by the most appalling row emerging from one of the houses. A couple were shouting abuse at one another at the top of their voices. The minister made straight for the offending dwelling and knocked loudly on the door. The noise ceased abruptly and the door was opened a fraction by the husband. 'Oh minister, it's you. Me an' Maggie were just havin' a bit crack afore we sat doon to oor tea. But come awa' in,' opening the door a further six uninviting inches.

In the kitchen a resentful Maggie did her best to put a face on things, even extending an invitation to join in the tea. 'No, no,' said the minister 'I'm not here for my tea. I just came to your door to see if I could stop that dreadful row you were making. You know, the pair of you could be heard half-way down the street. If you must disagree you should try and do it quietly. What was it you had got to fight about anyway? What was your disagreement?'

Said John, 'Ye've got it a' wrang, minister; there's nae disagreement between Maggie an' me.'

'Don't give me that,' said the minister. 'As I was saying half the village must have heard you yelling at one another. You were making a right laughing-stock of yourselves among all your neighbours. No disagreement can be worth that.'

'Am I no' tellin' you, minister,' said John, 'I can gi'e you my solemn word there's nae disagreement between Maggie an' me. I'll gi'e in to you we were hae'in a bit word thegither. You see I had juist opened my pay envelope an' there's four pound in it for overtime. Noo Maggie she thinks she's no' gettin' ony o' that. An' I think the same. No there's nae disagreement between us.'

The following tale of the young naval officer caught up in the toils of espionage is also in its way connected with big business and high finance – indeed it all turns upon the question of how high. I'm sure the hearer would not expect it to end as it does.

The young naval officer was reporting to his superior.

'In a pub last night,' he said, 'I was approached by a member of the Russian Intelligence and he was offering me £10,000 for a sight of the plans of our boom defences.'

'Dear me,' retorted the superior, 'and what did you do?'

'Sir, I stood to attention, I saluted, and I said, 'An officer in Her Majesty's Navy does not reveal the secrets of his country's defences for filthy lucre.' That settled him, sir, he didn't bother me any more.'

'Splendid,' said the senior man, 'well done indeed.'

Some little time later the young officer reported, 'The same Russian Intelligence man has been at me again about the plans of the home defences. This time he was offering £15,000.'

'And what did you do this time?'

'Sir, I stood to attention, I saluted and I said, "An officer in Her Majesy's Navy does not sell the secrets of his country's defences for filthy lucre." He went off with his tail between his legs, sir.'

It was perhaps a month later that the young officer presented himself with the news that he had been approached a third time, this time by a different contact, and that this time the offer had gone up to £20,000.

'So,' said the superior rather wearily, 'you stood to attention, you saluted and you said, "an officer in Her Majesty's Navy does not sell the secrets of his country's defences for filthy lucre".'

'That's right, sir; that's exactly what I did.'

'And why,' asked the senior man 'do you inist on coming and telling me all this when you appear to deal so adequately with it yourself?'

'Well, sir,' said the young officer, 'I thought you ought to know they're getting damn near my price.'

And what of the yarn about the little Chinese girl who was more than able for her would-be seducer. It has no real connection here except insofar as it rests upon the repudiation of a proposed deal. But in my view it's well worth telling.

She was a very pretty little Chinese girl and the beau was having a wonderful time chatting her up. He had been quite unsuccessful, however, in all his attempts to lure her up to his flat.

He found she was deeply interested when he got round to telling her of his unique collection of postage stamps. 'Why don't we pop up to my place and you can see them for yourself?' he hopefully proposed. 'No, no,' she replied, 'philately'll get you nowhere.'

The next one has nothing whatever to do with big business except that someone who could think so quickly in a situation must have been a real loss to big business.

There was quite a queue at the check-in desk at the Employment Exchange. The man who was being attended to affirmed that he was a baker. 'We've got a few openings for bakers . . .' The man behind counter was beginning when the unemployed man hastened to make clear, 'But I'm a seasonal worker, you see I only bake hot-cross buns.' He was duly enrolled for benefit and told to report for possible work nearer to Easter.

'And what is your occupation?' to the man next in the queue. 'Who, me? I'm a programme seller – a Coronation Programme seller.'

The Scots law of contract is an interesting affair. There are diverse ways in which a bargain may be completed so as to become binding upon the parties. For example, there is a provision about *rei interventus* whereby an incomplete contract can become binding if one of the parties, in good faith and within the kmowledge of the other party, acts upon the strength of it. I imagine that something of the kind must have been in the minds of the couple in this tale.

It was a Friday evening in the country village, and a wedding was in progress, or, more correctly, all was in readiness for a wedding. The trouble was that before setting off from home the bridegroom had forgotten to collect the Marriage Schedule from the Registrar. This official, it was learned after some furious phoning, was away for the weekend and could not be contacted.

The minister was adamant – no Schedule, no Wedding. There was nothing for it, therefore, but to have the ceremony postponed till Monday at earliest.

For the present, the minister suggested, the guests might proceed to the place appointed for the reception and enjoy the wedding-feast in anticipation – the boiled ham certainly wouldn't keep over the week-end.

When he returned to the vestry thinking he had now got things under control the minister was approached by bride and groom in a state of joint agitation. 'Look, minister, we've just been phoning the hotel where we're booked in for our honeymoon and they'll not change the date and they can't give us an extra room that would tide us over tonight. Could you not manage say a bit word that would be good enough for the two nights and we'd come back on Monday for the real thing.'

It's a very interesting situation and one with which I'm happy to say I have never been confronted.

In this section on business deals I think I might properly include the story of a transaction that involved a mule; but talking of mules reminds me of a lovely phrase I once heard. A friend was talking of a man of inordinate dourness – he was, he said, so stubborn that mules bowed to him in the street. It conjured up in my mind a picture of an Italian city basking in the mid-day sun, with a row of landau each drawn by a mule wearing a panama hat with holes cut out for its ears – my mental picture was of them all doffing their panamas as our friend walked down the street. But to our mule-centred transaction.

The man had just bought himself a mule. He had been a somewhat reluctant buyer for he understood that mules were mulish creatures and difficult to work. But the seller had assured him he would have no difficulty with this particular model. Provided he spoke to it quietly it would do whatever it was told. There was no point in shouting at it, still less in swearing at it; just speak to it quietly but firmly, letting it know what was expected of it and all would be well.

He had brought the animal home, fed it and bedded it, and now next morning he had got it out of the stable and into the yard, and not a thing could he get it to do. Speak to it in stern terms or wheedling whispers it just looked at him with dumb mulish insolence. Not unnaturally he got the seller on the phone and in terms of his warranty invited him to come and take his unmentionable creature away. That gentleman expressed profound surprise, but undertook to come over immediately. On arrival he took in the situation at a glance. Looking round the yard his eye fell on a length of broken shaft lying in a corner. Picking this up he walked up behind the animal and drew it a blow on the rump with this weapon that all but knocked it off its feet.

'But here,' remonstrated the buyer, 'you said I must always speak to it quietly.'

'That's right,' said the seller, 'but I thought you would understand, you've got to begin by capturing its attention.'

Could anyone possibly anticipate the sharp practice involved in 'The Tale of the Mink Weekend'?

A young fellow, accompanied by his positively luscious girl-friend, went into the shop of an extremely grand furrier where the young man explained to the assistant that he was seeking a fur wrap for his young lady. One item after another was rejected as the wrong size or the wrong shade, until finally, with the assistance of the manager himself, the shop's *pièce de resistance* was produced – a truly magnificent affair in chinchilla. This was draped over the lady's shoulders. She was enraptured. The young man was no less so. Ah yes, this was the very thing.

The young man seemed unperturbed when the manager reverently whispered in his ear the price of the Klondyke masterpiece. 'I'll just write you out a cheque for that,' the young man said.

'This is most awkward, sir, the manager replied in his most apologetic and obsequious manner. But you see this is a Friday afternoon and the banks are now closed for the weekend. Not that for a moment do I doubt your credit . . . but, well . . . a very large sum . . . one can't be too careful these days . . . you know how it is.

'Don't give it a thought. I perfectly understand. As a matter of fact you don't need to worry at all, for we're flying off in less than an hour's time for a weekend in the sun and Mimi here won't be wanting the wrap before we get back – will you, Darling?' The young lady whimpered her agreement. 'So what if I call in and collect on Tuesday afternoon. That will give you time to clear the cheque, wrap up the fur, and all will be ready for me to collect.'

On this harmonious note they parted. Came Tuesday and the young man returned. He was met by the manager with a face as long as the proverbial fiddle – indeed more like the length of a

211

cello – 'I'm terribly sorry to have to tell you, sir, that your cheque has bounced.'

'That doesn't surprise me a bit,' said the young man, 'I'd have been amazed if it hadn't. Just goes to prove how wise you were not to part with the fur. No, no, my only reason for looking in was to say thank you for your co-operation in securing me a weekend that has been simply out of this world.'

What's so funny in a poor defenceless young lassie being taken for a ride? Even if she hadn't a fur wrap to come home to.

CHAPTER FIFTEEN

BY WAY OF APOLOGY

THE FAITHFUL READER WHO HAS PERSEVERED thus far is doubtless suffering from exhaustion, if not exasperation, and thinks some sort of apology is called for. His complaint may, I imagine, take the form of three criticisms – that the argument has not been convincing, that there is not a single new joke in the whole of the book, and that the alleged jokes are not all that funny anyway.

Let me look at these points of criticism however briefly.

First that the argument has been less than convincing. This neither surprises nor disturbs me, for the philosophical aspect of the book was never intended to be taken too desperately seriously. The primary object of a book about mirth should surely be to entertain, and if the writer speaks sometimes with tongue in cheek what's wrong with that so long as it does not interfere with his diction – and subsequent digestion. If I have been successful in showing that there is in the subject of the humorous a matter worthy of careful study – if not of too serious study – then my own best hope has been fulfilled.

Secondly, the jokes are not new. This I freely admit. What I should really like to know is whether there is such a thing as a new joke. Is it not just that there are jokes that we haven't heard before? Occasionally in my hearing someone produces a joke preluded with the phrase, 'I've just heard this split new one.' As the tale unfolds I realise that although I haven't heard it for years I could with perfect honesty echo the sentiment of Jack Point's friend in The Yeomen – I've known that old joke from me cradle. Even when the detail and trappings of the tale have been altered (updated perhaps) the essential point of the story – what makes it 'tick' as a joke – is of real antiquity. Today's latest wisecrack about a jet plane may, who knows, have been told *mutatis mutandis* many years ago about the 'Flying Scotsman' – ay and centuries before that about an express stage-coach. To recount new jokes I have neither the ambition nor the ability – nor, come to that, the material!

Lastly that the stories are not all that funny anyway. Frankly I am more disturbed by this criticism, for as I read them in cold print I am inclined to agree. This state of affairs I should want to attribute to the fact that a joke is something meant to be told rather than read and the transition from the one medium to the other does it great harm. Regularly I have argued that public speakers do not on the whole pay sufficient attention to the differences in technique involved between making a speech and reading an essay. In no sphere, I am sure, is the distinction more acutely felt than in that of the humorous. There is a dramatic difference betweeen the speaker complete in dinner jacket and black tie standing at the top table and the same character draped in a white cloth lying on a mortuary slab. But the distinction is not so very much more dramatic than that between the story he tells in the cigar-smoke-laden atmosphere of the post- prandial party and the same joke written down on a cold white sheet of paper. A great deal of imagination needs to be contributed by the reader if a read joke is to retain its flavour. So if the reader has failed to find these jokes funny it may well be that the fault is as much his as it is mine. That, at least, is my defence and I'm sticking to it.

I think I might fairly sum it all up by saying that if I were to compose an epitaph for all that goes before it would read:

HIC IACET

*A Collection of Stories
most of which
sounded terribly funny
at the time*

LINDSAY PUBLICATIONS
PO BOX 812 GLASGOW G14 9NP
TEL/FAX 0141 569 6060
ISBN Prefix 1 898169

1 898169 00 4	*Scottish Home Baking*	Paterson	£4.95
03 9	*Scottish Home Cooking*	Paterson	£4.95
01 2	*Highland Dancing*	SOBHD	£10.00
08 X	*Glasgow's River*	Osborne	£9.99
06 3	*Homecraft*		£3.50
05 5	*Taste of Scotland*	Fitzgibbon	£8.99
10 1	*The Surgeon's Apprentice*	Young	£4.99
07 1	*Robert Burns*	Paterson	£4.50
12 8	*Savour of Scotland*	Morrison	£9.99
09 8	*Savour of Ireland*	Morrison	£9.99
11 X	*Lines Around the City*	Harvie	£10.99
13 6	*Still a Bigot*	Barclay	£4.99
14 4	*Happy Landings*	Barclay	£4.99
15 2	*Twisted Knickers & Stolen Scones*	Nicoll	£9.99
16 0	*Away with the Ferries*	Craig	£9.99
17 9	*Will I be Called an Author?*	Stuart	£7.99
23 3	*A Wheen O'Blethers*	Gray	£8.99
19 5	*Topsy & Tim aig an Dotair*	Adamson	£4.99
18 7	*T & T aig an Fhiaclair*	Adamson	£4.99
21 7	*T & T agus na Polis*	Adamson	£4.99
20 9	*T & T agus na Smaladairean*	Adamson	£4.99
24 1	*Oot the Windae*	Reilly	£6.99
22 5	*Laughing Matters*	Herron	£8.99